BARGELLO
TAPESTRY QUILTS
The Ultimate Quilt of the '90s

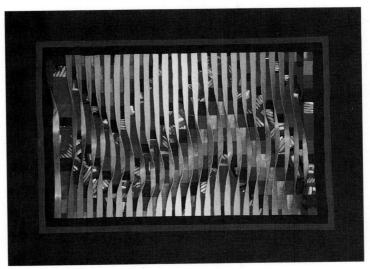

by Marilyn Doheny

Doheny Publications

Credits

Photography:	Mark Frey
Design and Illustrations:	Chuck Eng
Cover Design:	Chuck Eng
Additional illustrations, Production art:	G. Armour Van Horn

Front Cover *Turquoise Tapestry* by Diane Becka, page 44
Back Cover *Desert Palisades* by Shelley Nelson, page 57
Vacation Memories by Nell Moynihan, page 60
Title Page: *Amazing Grace* by Vivian Heiner, page 74

With loving memory for Mary Catherine Garvin

Bargello Tapestry Quilts
©1993 by Marilyn Doheny

Doheny Publications
P.O. Box 75
Edmonds, WA 98020

Published 1993. Second Edition 1994.
Printed in Hong Kong

Doheny, Marilyn
    Bargello Tapestry Quilts/Marilyn Doheny; [photography, Mark Frey; illustrations and graphics, Chuck Eng and G. Armour Van Horn].
    p. cm.
    ISBN 0-945169-12-4
    1. Quilting — Patterns. 2. Rotary Cutting — Patterns. I. Title

Library of Congress Catalog Card Number 92-076193

TABLE OF CONTENTS

ACKNOWLEDGEMENTS

With the most profound reverence and without being trite, I thank *the source of all creation.* To be specific and to start at the beginning of known memory, I thank:

My parents, Ellen Delehanty and Herbert Wellman who gave me life, (and kept me alive through adolescence) that I might in turn appreciate living.

My three children, Brielyn, Brendan, and Preston Doheny who are each a precious miracle and have, since their births, been the driving catalysts for my intense need to express myself, through artistic endeavors.

The quilt shop owners in Seattle, Washington who year after year encouraged my voracious teaching appetite by providing extensive teaching opportunities, Vickie McKenney, Mary Hales, Mary Collins, Sharon Yenter, Emily Nelson, Julie Petrezelka, Margaret Mathisson, and Donna Endressen.

My students/friends who never cease to amaze, encourage and inspire me by embracing my ideas and techniques wholeheartedly, producing exquisite "quilt art" and challenging me to give them even more, year after year.

To all the Bargello Tapestry students who generously offered their Bargello Tapestry Quilts to be professionally photographed and included in this book, enhancing its educational and inspirational values. You are especially appreciated and I hope honored with this publication.

Omnigrid™ owners, Randy and Peggy Schafer for responding to my ideas and incorporating my work into theirs, so that accuracy can be a reality.

Booth Managers/advisors/parents, "Papa Ed" Delehanty and Ellen Delehanty who travel with their personal spirit of love and enthusiasm, across the country, from one Quilt Symposium to another, promoting Cutting Edge Quilt Designs products with their hearts and souls.

Mark Frey, professional photographer and friend whose camera talent and patience created the essence of this book and whose friendship was so natural and intrinsic from the beginning, that I "knew" him, long before I actually met him.

Mary Fox, office manager, friend, second mother and outstanding quilter, who lovingly took over the business aspects of Cutting Edge Quilt Designs, affording me precious snatches of time for writing this book. I just want to ask you one thing Mary, "After all of the publishing expenses, is there any money left to buy fabric?"

Chuck Eng, for applying his creative efforts through endless graphic illustrations bringing these concepts to life in black and white.

Inquisitive friends and well-wishers — every anonymous one of you — who asked me, (*from the moment I began to write it*): "When this book would be finished?" Your questions were a constant reminder and challenge — all in the same breath — and they served to keep me focused and realize this goal. Amen!

Special Gratitude

To Janet Kime, my editor and my friend, for her infinite patience and work in bringing this manuscript "down the final stretch."

To Joel Patz for reviewing this manuscript for technical continuity, esthetic pleasure, and mostly so no one got embarrassed.

To Sue Pilarski and Connie Buss who "sewed strata" by the yards, hundreds of yards!!! I still have some strata "just waiting from these wonderful women," for more Bargello quilts.

To everyone who has a quilt in this book and does not recognize the name it was given by me. I thank you for your sense of humor while allowing my imagination to "fill in the blanks" when names were not supplied by the artist.

To two artists whose quilts have been used but whose names were misplaced in the shuffle of papers. Rather than omit these beautiful quilts, I identified them as: With Love from… a) Edmonds, b) Issaquah. (Let us know who you are for corrections before reprints are ordered.)

And last but not least, to you, dear reader, for being attracted to this book. Enjoy! This is the ultimate quilt book of the '90s

About Writing This Book

"Creativity is a part of your human spirit. It gives you joy, uniqueness and a key to the future if you will just allow it."
Jennifer James (1989)

In humor and sincerity, I want to ask the forgiveness of everyone who suffered through my various responses (over a two year period), to the inevitable question, "When will your Bargello Book be finished?." I would just like to say: Life as you now know it changes when you accept/ acquire the challenges of being a writer or author. There is a saying, "You either have results or reasons." And now, this book lives!

DEDICATION

I dedicate this book to two incredible women I admire very much. President and Director of Quilt Market, Karey Bresenhan for following her dream and establishing The International Quilt Market. Her vision and stamina continue to dramatically alter the history of quilting through unparalleled growth of the quilting industry.

Director of Education of International Quilt Market, Judy Murrah, for supporting my teaching efforts by giving me the larger audience I was seeking, nationally and internationally.

And finally, to the profound level of Creative Intelligence in each of us. May we live in the awareness of our connectedness to this universal source.

C H A P T E R   1

INTRODUCTION

> "The question is," said Alice, "whether you *can* make words mean so many different things."
>
> "The question is," said Humpty Dumpty, "which is to be master—that's all."
>
> — *Through the Looking Glass*

Bargello and *tapestry* have not been quilting terms until now. I have borrowed the term "Bargello" from the world of needlepoint and the term "Tapestry" from its historical meaning of richly detailed woven cloth. The terms are combined to describe the undulating richness of the quilts in this book and the unique and innovative methods for creating them.

Years ago I was inspired by a Bargello pillow on a friend's couch. My eyes were attracted to the waves of color, and I was intrigued by the idea of creating such designs in fabric. I could immediately see how I could use strata techniques to create the foundation for Bargello Tapestry patterns using fabrics.

That was hundreds of Bargello Tapestry quilts ago. I was tantalized by the flowing motions of each Bargello quilt I created, and found something new to try with each successive quilt. I discovered that Bargello designs can be soft and billowy or steep and piercing. I found that there are an infinite number of effects that can be achieved by altering the fabric selection, the width of the fabric strips, and the motion of the colors. Each design was more exciting than the last.

The knowledge gained from my efforts and those of my students are presented in this book. Using your own fabrics and the design units provided in the instructions, you will be able to create your own spectacular Bargello Tapestry quilts, brimming with undulating rhythm. Each will be a unique masterpiece.

Don't be intimidated by the quilts in this book. The overall appearance of every Bargello Tapestry quilt is complex, yet the pattern is very simple, composed entirely of squares and rectangles. There are only two technical skills necessary: cutting a straight line and sewing a straight seam. That's it, cutting and sewing straight lines.

Many of the quilts in this book were created by my students, some of whom were beginning quilters. All of the designs are the result of different fabric combinations and different Bargello Tapestry design elements. You will be able to create beautiful flowing motion with each and every one of your efforts. The techniques will encourage your own artistic expression; the creative opportunites are profound.

This book will show you how to use different design elements to create your own mesmerizingly beautiful Bargello Tapestry quilts. All of the designs and techniques are simple; the only complexity is the appearance of every Bargello quilt—intriguing and breathtaking all at once. The possibilities for expressing your creativity in a Bargello Tapestry quilt are infinite. Get ready for the compliments and awards for your efforts!

C H A P T E R 2

HOW TO USE THIS BOOK

This is not a pattern book. It's much better than that! It is the definitive book of infinite Bargello designs. You will learn the basic techniques of making a variety of Bargello Tapestry effects, which can be used alone or in combination with one another to create an infinite number of stunning tapestry quilts. Chapter 12, **Strata Math** will help you calculate yardages and plan the size of your quilt—there are no instructions for exactly duplicating the movement and pattern for any of the quilts in the color gallery. The composition and yardage, however, are provided in Appendix B for each quilt photographed. Each Bargello Tapestry quilt you make will involve personal and delightful choices. Let the photographs guide and inspire you. Learn to create as you go rather than know everything at the beginning.

There are two ways to begin: by trying one of the six techniques identified and working on a small project, or by diving into the complete instructions for all six variations to get well grounded in the entire subject matter. Follow **Getting Your Feet Wet** for the quicker approach in Chapter 4, or **The Deep Dive** for the more studious approach, by reading the entire book first. Either way, remember to have fun with your fabrics!

GETTING YOUR FEET WET

Find one photographed quilt that delights you with its flowing colors, values and prints. Read the information that is needed for that style Bargello alone. Read Chapter 4 for a bit of guidance. Create the strata unit that resembles your choice. Tube the strata by sewing the first and last fabrics together, make some counter-cuts of varying widths, and arrange them into a similar pattern of upward and downward movement. You will immediately see (1) how easy Bargello movement is to create and (2) how many different possibilities there are with just one strata unit. This first attempt will provide you with marvelous and immediate gratification, and you will learn quickly about the basic technique from your hands-on experience. Any problems, difficulties or questions that arise are covered in **The Deep Dive**.

Some of my students prefer experimenting with different design elements on their own. Other students want specific directions on how to achieve particular effects. If you are like these students and you want more information, it is time for . . .

THE DEEP DIVE

The deep dive is an extensive study of each aspect of Bargello Tapestry design style. Read the sections on tools and techniques and fabric selection to give yourself a solid foundation. Familiarize yourself with the terms used in this book. Study the basic design effects and their illustrations to understand the different techniques. Study the instructions and illustrations for each type of movement, curve, and point. Read through the design sections until you have a good understanding of how each effect is achieved. You may then want to get your feet wet and experiment with an individual design element, or try combining different elements. You can make small projects, wall hangings or lap quilts, from your first experiments. As you can see from the size of the quilts in this book, a Bargello Tapestry quilt doesn't have to be large to be stunning!

With only a little practice, you will have the confidence to plan and execute a large project involving many fabrics and design elements. Larger is not more difficult — larger is simply more seams to sew and something that takes up more space and time and is bigger when it's done!

ROTARY CUTTING TOOLS AND TECHNIQUES

I f you are not already using rotary cutting equipment, you will want to invest in these tools for your Bargello Tapestry quilts. They will increase both speed and accuracy in all of your fabric-cutting efforts.

You must have at least three items to rotary cut your fabric:

1. *Rotary cutter*—a round, sharp blade in a hand-held plastic tool. A rotary cutter looks like a rolling pizza cutter. You expose the blade manually and press it down into the fabric. As you pull or push the tool across the cloth, the blade rolls and cuts the fabric.
2. *Cutting board*—a specially designed, self-healing mat that protects the floor or table surface as you cut, and also helps to keep the blade from dulling quickly.
3. *Ruler*—a clear acrylic ruler used as a guide along which the blade rolls for straight, precise cuts.

BRANDS

Quality is most important to me in any investment I make. Products and their parts must be durable and dependable. They must function as advertised and assist my quiltmaking efforts, not interfere with them. There are competitive brands on the market for all of these tools. The prices, features, and quality vary with each. Poor quality tools are often less expensive but are a waste of money; they can be dangerous and can hinder your progress and success.

I recommend the following:

Olfa® rotary cutters and replacement blades
Olfa® cutting mats exclusively
Omnigrid™ rulers exclusively

My years as a professional quilter and teacher support these suggestions. Each product listed is durable, dependable, versatile, and *accurate.* They are made with the best materials on the market and stand up to the demands of precision work, project after project, year after year.

Inferior tools offer a world of disappointment in return for your investment. If the lines, numbers, and angles on rulers and mats are inaccurate, you cannot help making errors as you cut. Some cutters advertise safety features that are actually hazardous, some are shaped so that your strength is not applied directly over the blade and you must work harder, and some will push against your carefully layered fabric and shift it. Inferior products wear out quickly and are often packaged with flaws.

If you already own equipment that is not Olfa® or Omnigrid™, try to upgrade to these products as soon as possible. You will immediately appreciate the difference in quality. If the collective price of these items is prohibitive, you might go in with a friend and share the cutting mat and rulers. Do not try to share a rotary cutter; I have seen friendships strained over cutters that were returned with dull or nicked blades. Use a permanent marker to identify each of your items with your name. In a classroom, your equipment can easily be confused with someone else's.

The purchase of high quality cutting equipment is an investment in yourself as well as your work. The time and effort you spend in creating a quilt are very valuable. Good equipment will save time, increase accuracy, and will last for many years.

"Take care in what you do — show that you have pride in you!"

FABRIC PREPARATION
■ Washing — dye removal
Pre-wash your fabric if you wish, to remove formaldehyde and excess dye. Do not use harsh soaps (choose ones you would bathe in). Use Orvis Paste for the kindest treatment of the cloth. It is not necessary to wash light-color fabrics.

■ Ironing — shrinkage
Before you cut the fabric strips, it is very important to steam-iron the fabric to shrink it and eliminate all wrinkles. It isn't necessary to wash your fabric to shrink it; the steam-ironing will do the job. Think about it: steam is boiling water — the hottest water temperature there is — hotter than anything in your washer and dryer.

■ Spray starch — strengthen and control
If necessary, use a fabric spray starch, then steam iron to stiffen and strengthen. It works wonders on loosely woven cloth or rayon blends if you use spray starch before cutting the strips.

■ Metallic Fabrics
Iron on a fusible webbing (interfacing) to the wrong side of metallic fabrics to secure their edges before cutting the strips. Be careful and use a pressing cloth. Hot irons melt metallic tissue lamè.

Figure 3-1

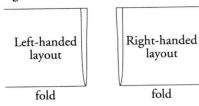

Left-handed layout

Right-handed layout

fold

fold

Figure 3-2

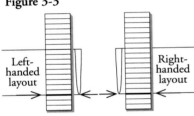

A.

B.

Figure 3-3

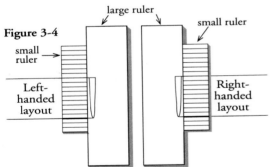

Left-handed layout

Right-handed layout

CUTTING THE STRATA STRIPS

■ The clean-up cut

All fabric should be placed with the folded edge by your tummy so that your eyes can look straight down on the folded edge, not at an angle to it. If the selvedges are closest to you and the fold farther away, you have a distorted view of the fold. Right-handed people should have the excess fabric on the right, left-handed people should have it on the left (trust me here) (Fig. 3-1). You will need two rulers; one can be smaller than the other.

■ Get acquainted terms and ruler usage

On each ruler there are two sets of lines: short lines (edge to edge) (Figure 3-2A), and long lines (end to end)(Figure 3-2B).

1. Position the smaller ruler first by placing a short line on the fold, with the entire ruler lying on the cloth near the cut end (Figure 3-3). Use a line and not the end of the ruler, because the end of the acrylic ruler is just glare and difficult to position accurately.

2. Hold the small ruler in this position with your cutting hand.

3. With your other hand, place the longer ruler up against the short ruler (Figure 3-4).

4. Press down on the longer ruler so it will stay in position, and

5) Pick up and remove the shorter ruler with your cutting hand (Fig. 3-5). Using this method, you establish a line at 90° to the fold on the outside edge of the fabric.

Figure 3-4

large ruler

small ruler

small ruler

Left-handed layout

Right-handed layout

Figure 3-5

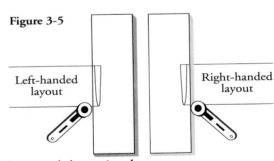

Left-handed layout

Right-handed layout

6. Do not cut until you have read the entire chapter.

If this first cut is not at 90° to the fold, (i.e., if you don't cut perpendicular to the fold), when you open your strip you will have what I call a "dog leg" or kink at the folded area rather than a straight strip (Figure 3-6). If you don't have a straight strip it is very difficult to sew a straight line. It is also important to have only one fold in your fabric, or

Figure 3-6

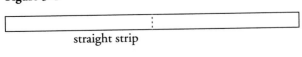

straight strip

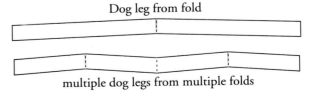

Dog leg from fold

multiple dog legs from multiple folds

you'll have multiple dog legs!

If you make your clean-up cut in this manner, you will not have to move your fabric or move to the other side of the table to make your cuts. It is also an excellent reason to buy an Omnigrid™ ruler if you don't already have one. You can keep the ruler you have and use it to position the Omnigrid™ ruler for clean-up cuts. Use the Omnigrid™ ruler for all of the accurate strip cutting.

■ Cutting multiple layers of fabric

You can stack your fabrics and cut several layers at the same time, if you take care to place each fold parallel to the others. There are three fantastic advantages to the layering method: time saved, accuracy, and safety.

CUTTING MULTIPLE LAYERS IS FASTER: If I have two fabrics and I cut 10 strips from each, one at a time, I have repeated the same effort 20 times. If I stacked the two fabrics I would need to make only 10 cuts to get 20 strips. If I stacked four layers, I would need to make only five cuts to get 20 strips. The wear and tear on the blade and on my arms and elbows and wrists is greatly decreased, as is the possibility of cutting myself.

To save even more time, I usually cut my strips with the fabrics layered together in their actual sewing order. This saves organizing them into their sewing order later. Make a common clean-up cut to all of the fabrics at the same time, after they are layered.

CUTTING MULTIPLE LAYERS IS SAFER AND MORE ACCURATE: Multiple-layer cuts are also more accurate. If I have to make 20 different cuts, they could be 20 slightly different widths. The fewer cuts, the less variation there will be in the width of my strips. Also, since I am expending the energy required for five cuts rather than 20, I won't get as fatigued cutting all the strips for a quilt and can focus better and concentrate more on making accurate cuts.

Those of you who are intimidated by cutting multiple layers for any reason should relax. These blades are surgical steel, and can cut through up to 16 layers of fabric with no problem. In fact, the cutter works better and more accurately on a thick stack of fabric than on individual fabrics.

To use an analogy, if you take a large meat cleaver and head toward a lemon merengue pie, you will go through not only the pie and the crust but through the pie tin and into the counter as well. The meat cleaver is far too large a tool for the job. Taking a large rotary cutting blade and cutting through only one fabric (two layers) is like cutting a lemon merengue pie with a meat cleaver—you have no sense of the fabric being there at all. With no sensation that you are cutting through anything, it is very easy to wander and miscut. If on the other hand there are several layers of fabric, the cutting sensation is like thick, soft fudge. The blade is not inhibited, but the sensation of thickness helps you to guide the cutter and you will be much less likely to wander with the cutter. You can feel the fabric, and will be able to cut more accurately and will be much less likely to cut yourself.

Try cutting three or four fabrics layered together. Since each fabric is folded once, this will be six or eight layers of fabric (Fig. 3-7). Build up to a point where you can cut six, seven, or even eight fabrics, up to 16 layers.

NOTE: Beyond 16 layers it is difficult to cut because the disk of the rotary cutter tends to ride on top of the ruler and won't allow you to

Figure 3-7

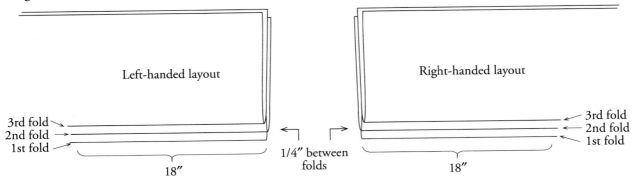

Left-handed layout   Right-handed layout

3rd fold
2nd fold
1st fold

3rd fold
2nd fold
1st fold

1/4" between folds

18"   18"

penetrate any deeper.

ON CUTTING

■ Use an Olfa® brand cutter with multilayer stacks

The Olfa® cutters take on stacked fabrics with no interference. The only cutter that has trouble with multiple layers of fabric is the tension-retractable Dritz® cutter. The guard on the Dritz® cutter is pushed back by the fabric as you cut to expose the blade. This particular cutter does not work well with layered fabrics. The guard of the Dritz® cutter pushes into the fabric layers and shoves them around just as if you had pushed your finger into the stack and shoved it or dragged it.

■ Stack the fabrics carefully

As you stack the fabrics, keep the folds parallel. To do this, lay out the first fabric and position it about ½" up from the edge of the mat. The next fabric should be placed with its fold parallel but ¼" above the first fold. Keep the folds parallel for up to 18". Place the next fabric with the fold about ¼" above the previous fold and so on until the fabrics get within ½" of the top of the mat. Stop there. (Fig. 3-7)

After you have stacked (staggered) four or five fabrics, the selvedges may travel off the upper edge of the mat. Do not let the stack get taller than your 24" ruler. If it is taller than 24", you will have to move your ruler to complete the cut and it will be difficult to maintain accuracy. Rather than run the stack taller than 24", position the fabrics at ⅛" intervals rather than ¼" next time around.

■ Cut with your strength

You can start cutting at the folds and push your cutter away from your tummy toward the top of the fabric, or start cutting at the top edges (selvedges) and pull the cutter toward you from the top of the mat. *It doesn't matter.* I know this is a bone of contention with many people, but everyone should cut in the direction of their natural inclination—which is to cut *with* your strength.

You may find you have much more control and can cut more safely pulling the blade toward you rather than pushing it out into space. It is a much more controllable way to cut, but I know many of you have been taught to cut away from yourself with sharp objects. I'd like you to consider the possibility of change. If in fact you cut away from yourself and you are pleased with the effect of the cutting, meaning you don't miscut at the beginning or end of the cut, then by all means continue to cut away from your tummy, away from yourself. But if you have had some trouble with your cutting try starting at the selvedges and pulling the cutter toward you.

Figure 3-8

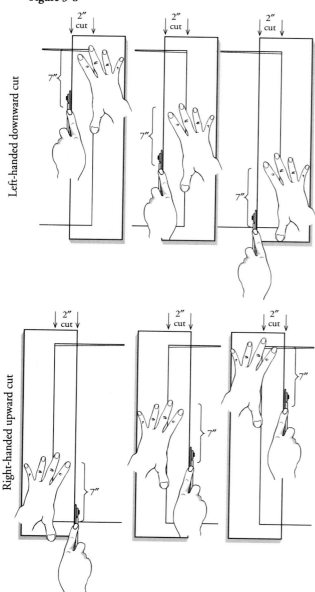

Left-handed downward cut

Right-handed upward cut

■ Holding the ruler—"Inchworming"

Move your hand down the ruler as you cut. Regardless of whether you cut away from or toward yourself, it is imperative that you do two things:

a) Keep the cutter against the edge of the ruler as you cut.

b) Have your opposite hand holding the ruler where you are actually cutting at all times. You must learn to move your hand down (or up) the ruler as you cut. I call the movement *inchworming.* This is done in 6 to 8 inch intervals depending on your finger spread.

c) As I cut, the hand holding my ruler is perched on the fingers. I spread my fingertips and thumb far apart and my hand is perched on all of my finger pads rather than having my palm rest flat on the ruler. This allows my wrist, elbow, and shoulder to rotate freely during the cutting. Do not plant your palm flat; it is very restrictive and forces your body weight and joint rotations to be very ineffective.

As I cut along the edge of the ruler, the distance I cut is about 7″ from my fingertips to my thumb tip. I then stop the cutting motion and inchworm the ruler hand.

To inchworm, I bring my fingertips to my thumb and move my thumb lower, and continue to cut for another 7″. My hand never leaves the ruler. I travel down my ruler in three or four inchworm movements (Figure 3-8).

Those of you who cut away from yourselves will inchworm the thumb up to the fingers and then reposition the fingers higher.

Figure 3-9
Optional left-handed downward cut

OPTION: If this inchworming movement is difficult because of arthritis, carpal tunnel syndrome, or past broken bones, you can cut for the distance of your finger spread: *Put the cutter down,* place your cutting hand on the ruler to hold it while you reposition the ruler hand up or down to the next area, pick up the blade and cut another 7″ distance.

Whichever method you use to reposition your hand, hold the ruler firmly. Don't cut against a ruler edge unless you are holding the ruler at that location. If you attempt to cut against the ruler at a place where your hand isn't holding the ruler, the ruler will pivot (slip and slide) and you will miscut your strips and possibly cut yourself in the process.

1. Make first area of the cut.

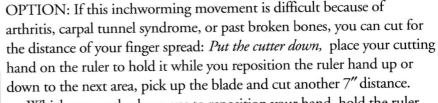

■ Make additional clean-up cuts as necessary to maintain accuracy

After a few strips have been cut parallel to the long outside edge, move the ruler in so it lies entirely on the fabric. Position one of the short lines of the ruler on the fabric fold and check to see if the long outside edge of the fabric is still at a 90° angle (Figure 3-10). If it isn't, use a second ruler to hold the correct 90° edge, remove the first ruler, and make another clean-up cut. See Figures 3-4 and 3-5.

2. Set cutter aside.

3. Put the cutting hand on the ruler.

4. Move ruler hand down to next position.

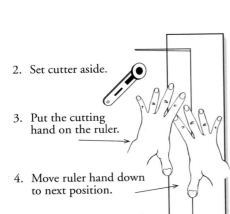

Figure 3-10

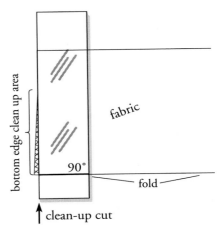

5. Pick up the cutter.

6. Make the next area of the cut.

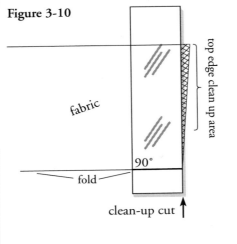

NOTE: For cutting away from yourself, reverse this sequence.

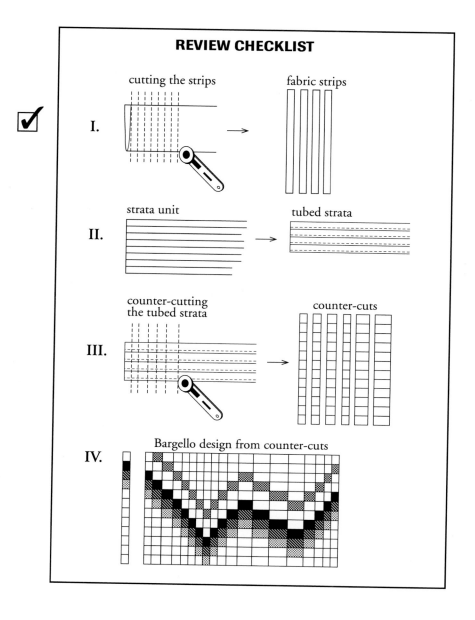

REVIEW CHECKLIST

I. cutting the strips → fabric strips

II. strata unit → tubed strata

III. counter-cutting the tubed strata → counter-cuts

IV. Bargello design from counter-cuts

C H A P T E R   4

INTRODUCTION TO BARGELLO CONSTRUCTION

This chapter provides a brief overview of the steps required to construct a Bargello Tapestry quilt. *This chapter does not provide all the information you need to make a Bargello Tapestry quilt.* There is a great deal of information in the following chapters on fabric selection and strata construction that will ensure the success of your quilt. You may want to get your feet wet by making a strata unit, counter-cutting it, and arranging the counter-cuts into a Bargello Tapestry design, but don't commit yourself to a major project until you have read the rest of the book. There are many strata styles to choose from.

Use this chapter as a step-by-step review as you make each Bargello Tapestry quilt.

1. Select an array of beautiful fabrics and arrange them in an attractive flow based on value gradations. See Chapter 5, **Fabric Selection** for detailed information.

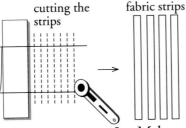

Figure 4-1
cutting the strips

fabric strips

Figure 4-2 strata unit

22"   22"

44"

2. Make cuts of each fabric **at the desired width,** approximately 45″ long (Figure 4-1). For options of widths, see Chapter 6, Strata Planning.

3. Create **strata units** by sewing the fabric strips together along their long edges (Figure 4-2).Chapter 7, Strata Construction, has excellent guidelines for sewing accurately.

4. Steam-iron the seam allowances so that they lie smooth and flat and flow in one direction in each strata unit. **Half of the total number of strata units should be ironed up and half down.** If only one strata unit is created, cut it into two equal 22″ units. Iron the first unit up and iron the second unit down. Ironing details are covered extensively in Chapter 7, **Strata Construction.**

5. Check and correct the strata units: look for any distortions or inconsistencies and correct them. For details of natural problems and corrective measures, see Chapter 8, **Tubing the Strata and Counter-Cutting.**

6. Remove the selvedges at both ends of the strata unit, making clean-up cuts at a 90° angle to a central internal seam (Figure 4-3).

Figure 4-3

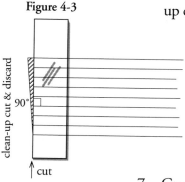

Figure 4-4

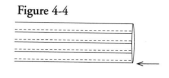

7. Create a tube by sewing the first and last strips in the strata unit together along their long edges, for the distance that they lay parallel on a seam and do not twist (Figure 4-4). If the strata unit begins to twist or the strips lose their parallel alignment, refer to **Check and Correct** in Chapter 8, **Tubing the Strata and Counter-Cutting.**

8. Make perpendicular counter-cuts into each strata tube, and alternate between two tubes which are ironed in opposite directions when counter-cutting so that the direction of the seam allowances alternates with each counter-cut in the overall design (Figure 4-5). Details of motion development are in Chapters 10 and 11.

Figure 4-5

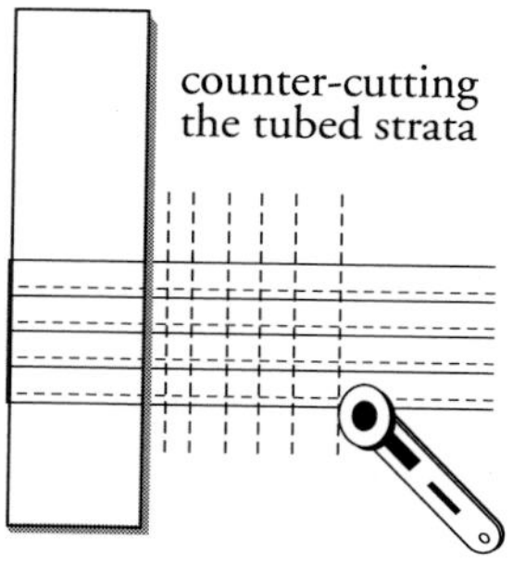

counter-cutting the tubed strata

Figure 4-6

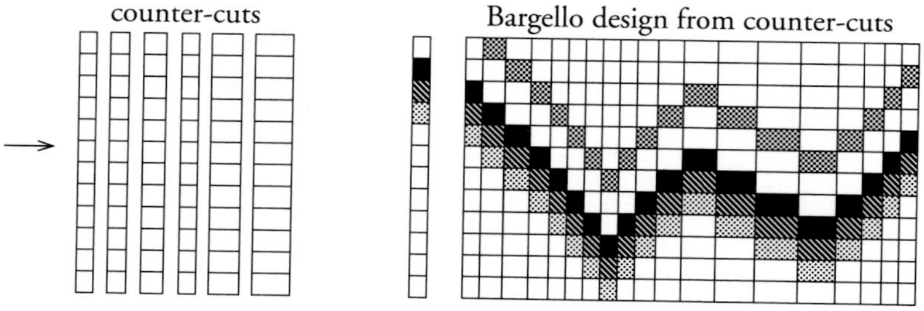

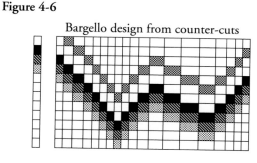

counter-cuts

Bargello design from counter-cuts

9. Open each counter-cut, removing the desired seam. See Chapter 9, **Strata Into Bargello Motion.**

10. Add each counter-cut to the design(Figure 4-6).

11. Sew the counter-cuts together.

12. As the quilt is designed, it will appear to be 45" wide for every strata unit used, but when seams are taken it will reduce considerably; to approximately 22″ to 28″ per strata used.

13. When you border, be sure the corners of the quilt are at 90° angles. If not, trim to be so.

14. Quilt as desired.

15. Bind.

C H A P T E R   5

FABRIC SELECTION

Each Bargello Tapestry quilt is an integrated orchestration of many fabrics. Each quilt has its own unique harmony and rhythm. When you look at a Bargello Tapestry quilt you can feel the music and see the numerous fabrics dancing. Your heart takes a leap!

If each fabric in a Bargello Tapestry quilt could sing, you would not hear individual voices but a celestial choir. It is important that no individual fabric should stand out as a soloist. This chapter will explain how to select a magnificent choir of fabrics for a Bargello Tapestry quilt. The next chapter on Strata Planning will help you arrange the colors, values, and textures into a complex and magnificent whole.

Fabric selection is a very emotional process. Although I am going to give you clear guidelines to help you plan a stunning Bargello quilt, nothing is as important as your own heartfelt fabric selection. The fabrics and their relationship to one another are the heart and soul of a quilt, and they must reflect the heart and soul of the creator. Use both your head and your heart as you select your fabric. The close-contrast guidelines will help you arrange *any* fabrics into a wonderful choir that works together.

MY APPROACH TO FABRIC SELECTION

To understand my approach to selecting and purchasing fabric, it will help if I first explain how I feel about fabric. I adore it. Just seeing it excites me and inspires a fresh flow of ideas. I can't keep from touching fabric when I see it. If I were less self-conscious, I'm sure I would unroll beautiful new bolts of cloth right in the store, lay down on the fabric, and wrap myself up in it and roll around. I am absolutely passionate about fabric.

All of my fabric purchases are emotional. I simply love selecting and owning fabric. The fabrics I buy go home with me and become shelf stock, to be considered and used sometime in the future. Keep in mind (1) I purchase fabric to own it, not necessarily to use it, and (2) I rarely purchase fabric for a specific quilt or project; I'm actually collecting paint for my quilter's paintbox.

As a quilter, fabrics are my voice to the world. Whatever moods, emotions, or feelings I want to convey, fabric is my preferred medium of expression. I even dream about fabric textures, colors, and patterns. I'm a gushy, passionate person and therefore I prefer to have a large number of fabrics working together to achieve a desired effect, rather than rely on only a few to convey my message. Fabrics are the paint in my paintbox, and I purchase and use them freely.

■ **Purchasing fabric — My approach is this: if I see it, I buy it.**
Before you decide I'm the most decadent woman in the world with endless finances, let me explain this method. It is a bona fide method, even though it seems very indulgent and loose!

"If I see it, I buy it," *is* a sophisticated approach to fabric selection, and one that has taken me time to fully appreciate. If a fabric catches my eye among all the fabrics in the store (500 to over 2,000 bolts)—that means I like it! I let unconscious evaluations select my fabric. I never question my first response; I never try to think about what or how I will use the fabric, or whether I have anything to use with it. My choices are spontaneous. I believe everyone's unconscious mind is full of complex interaction and this alone is the best guide to selecting fabrics.

The emerging artist in each of us needs to be spontaneous; you can use this approach delightfully, effectively and effortlessly. Just look around and gather together the attractive bolts, at least 30 to 60. Then let your intellect narrow down the selection if money is an issue. *Go to every color section in the store.* Customers refile bolts and you will often find reds in with the browns, greens with the yellows, a wild array of blues and greens mixed together, purples in with blues and blacks and so on!

■ **Using a fabric or color as a starting place**
There are other, more intellectual ways to select fabric. They involve consulting something that already exists: a wallpaper swatch, a bedspread, an armchair cover, another piece of fabric, a photograph from nature or of an existing quilt. Some quilters need a jumping-off point, from which they can start pulling bolts and making fabric stacks. Try to avoid, however, allowing an item or an idea to dictate all your fabric choices. I am always disappointed when I see a quilt artist (and we are all artists) under the rigid control of an inanimate object. *Use an object to set the stage, not to direct the show.* Look at the object then put it away (consult it every 30 minutes if necessary), but always put it away in-between times—your fabric selection will be richer for it. Have a rich array—not a perfect match.

■ **How much should you buy?**
I buy anything from ½ yard to 6 yards, or occasionally the whole bolt, depending only on how much I like the fabric. I pull the bolt off the shelf and look at the fabric, and assess the increase in my heart rate and

salivary glands. This approach is more fun and certainly faster than any other. Lots of saliva and heavy breathing is worth six yards of fabric. Dilation of my pupils and a rapid heart rate is good for one to three yards. Just seeing a fabric is always worth one-half yard.

How much should *you* buy? You'll have to assess your own heart rate and budget! But I recommend never less than ½ yard. If your approach to fabric selection is more methodical than mine, you can use **Strata Math** Chapter 12, to determine the yardage you will need for each fabric in the Bargello Tapestry quilt you are planning, and purchase that much.

■ Where do I buy my fabrics?

Mostly where I teach—in stores across the USA as well as the terrific stores in Seattle, Edmonds, Poulsbo, and Stanwood in Washington state. **I suggest that everyone shop at the stores that they most want to see stay in business!**

COMBINING FABRICS

I think fabrics work best when combined. For me, fabrics need each other to sing a full song in a quilt, and this is especially true with a Bargello Tapestry quilt. The more the merrier and the richer the visual effect.

Each quilt project requires different fabric considerations. The possible combinations of fabric and diverse arrangements within a design are infinite. Unless you want to go insane considering the possibilities, some decisions must be made, and that means some fabrics must be eliminated. Or plan to make hundreds of Bargello quilts, playing out numerous artistic considerations.

■ Defining the mood of your quilt

Determine the desired mood of each project. To help focus your fabric selection, close your eyes and visualize the way you want the quilt to affect the viewer. Do you want a casual, fun, and frivolous look, or one that is tailored and disciplined? Do you like a masterfully artistic or a romantic, graceful effect? Should the quilt be subdued or flamboyant? Should it be youthful and gay, or mature and sophisticated? Should it be more masculine or more feminine? Define the mood you want your quilt to evoke. Once you have this mood in mind, it will help you select the fabrics that comply. Once you identify the goal, finding the fabrics to do the job is quick and fun. Plaids are casual, solids are subdued, florals are romantic, paisleys are rich, stripes are zesty, and so on!

■ Gathering the candidates

My extensive fabric stash occupies some part of each room in my office. It lies waiting, neatly folded on shelves (somewhat), tables (often, but not folded), and in piles on the floor (where it fell off the tables and shelves).

I never have all of my fabrics together — it would be impossible. No room in my office is that large! I'm not that controlled!

I think of a mood or effect, or let a single fabric inspire me. I quickly grab fabrics which catch my eye. I make no attempt to match, coordinate, or arrange them. I always begin by gathering together 30 or more fabrics. This first gathering is very quick, and entirely spontaneous and emotional. My only rule is to try and have a range of darks, mediums, and lights, with no regard for gathering equal amounts of each value in colors that I desire.

If you don't have a large fabric stash to work from, you can use the same process in a fabric store. Walk about the fabric bolts and act like a child in a candy store, with no restrictions. Walk through every color section and, with a casual eye, look at all of the different values and print styles. When something catches your eye, take that bolt off the shelf. Don't try to match a wallpaper swatch or paint chip; don't try to match fabrics as you go; don't try to match anything! Some of the fabrics may be rejected later or others may be specifically sought out and added to the group to round out the primary selection. You will end up with a group of fabric that is rich and exciting. This is better than a controlled and boring collection, which is what usually results from trying to match a pre-existing item.

Figure 5-1

Keep pulling bolts until you have at least 30. Arrange the bolts like books on a shelf, side by side. Back up 6-10 feet and view them as a collective whole (Figure 5-1). You should have a diverse array of:

a) values (dark, medium, and light),

b) at least two distinct color families (you can use one family only but two creates more visual excitement),

c) some large-scale prints as well as small-scale prints

d) solids, and

e) some prints that have what I call a double voice. A *double-voice* fabric has at least two different colors or values that appear in different areas of the pattern, so that a 1″ square cut from one area is a completely different color or value from a 1″ square cut from another area of the same cloth. This can be color-related as in red and blue areas, or value-related as in dark and light areas.

Once a large selection of fabrics are represented in your collection, go ahead and buy some of each fabric. If you have preplanned your quilt size and yardage requirements, follow your calculations. You can rely upon the yardage requirements associated with the photographs of the quilts in this book. (See *Yardage and Cutting Information* in Appendix B.) If you haven't planned your quilt yet, buy ½ yard (or ¼ yard, if that is all your budget will allow) of each fabric and be assured of having enough and then some! The final selection and organization of fabric for your quilt will happen at home.

■ **Selection requires assortment.**

Selecting and arranging fabric is very personal and individualistic. Some of us are cautious while others are more radical; we each have a different head and heart. You may, however, be inspired by something in nature or another artist's work. Consider yourself an apprentice to that source for color and composition. This is a compliment to the source, whoever or whatever it is. Examine the colors, textures, and patterns for subtleties and determine what you like and what you would change. Proceed toward your own creation and enjoy the choices you make along the way. I believe that the primary joy of any quilt is the *experience* of creating it. Notice contrasts too—colors by other colors, values and textures— side by side. Contrast large, medium and small scale patterns.

NOTE: If there are similarities between your quilt and the work that inspired it, it is always fair and rewarding to give written credit to your source of inspiration when showing your quilt. If a sunset or a rose inspired you, send a kiss on the wind to Mother Earth and the sun!

■ **The 10% risk factor**

I recommend that you include a 10% risk factor in your fabric selection process. Most of the fabrics selected should reflect your current level of attraction and comfort, but include some fabrics you would not normally choose. Risky fabrics could be darker or lighter than you normally prefer, or large-scale prints that go beyond your norm, or a color mix that is new for you, perhaps allowing purple to be in with the blues.

By 10% risk, I mean that you are 90% content and confident with your fabric selection, and 10% uncomfortable. If you are very *uncomfortable*, you have taken more than a 10% risk and you need to back up a little. You should have a risky sense of play and excitement when you look at your stack, but definitely not fright! On the other hand, if you are very *comfortable* and satisfied with your fabric selection, you did not take a full 10% risk. Add a little more risk and excitement to your selection!

Did I hear you say you don't know what your quilt will look like? . . . Well, good! If you knew what your quilt would look like there would be no creative excitement involved in making it. There would be very little excitement left to entice you to finish it. Eventually the quilt would bore you, perhaps even before you cut it out!

Using the 10% risk factor will help you grow and develop as an artist with each quilt you plan. When you design with cloth, you transform the material into something new—and as you change the cloth, the cloth changes you. You'll find yourself becoming more adventuresome. You'll find yourself cruising areas of the fabric store that you avoided before. And you'll be surprised at how a 10% risk factor will spark up your quilts too! Let go a little and feel the passion, risk, and excitement of creativity — and the joy of unexpected surprises. You will astound your friends who think they know what to expect from your fabric choices. Admirers will think you have an art degree—that you *knew* what you were doing!

■ Fabric selection checklist

The richness and harmony of a Bargello Tapestry quilt are the result of many fabrics working together. This overall effect of richness is the key to the quilt having a tapestry-like lushness. Eventually, you will gain confidence in selecting fabrics for Bargello Tapestry quilts and will freely enjoy combining a wide range of fabrics. At first, however, you will probably need the list of suggestions below. Use them to evaluate your spontaneous selection of fabrics, adding and subtracting fabrics as you discover any weak areas.

Arrange your fabrics in a group with an equal amount of each fabric showing. Stand back about 10 feet and ask yourself the following questions:
1. Are there at least two fabrics of each value—dark, medium, and light?
2. Are there at least three large "active" prints?
3. Are at least two distinct colors represented?
4. Does any individual fabric stand out from the rest? (Then it needs a friend or partner.)

VALUE: There should be at least two dark, two medium, and two light fabrics somewhere in your selection. *You do not need to have equal proportions of darks, mediums, and lights.* A range that includes all values will enrich and enliven all your fabrics and give a sensation of depth to your selection. If all values are not present in your quilt the effect is flat and mushy; it has no depth or aliveness. I call it "paste." Avoid creating visual paste!

PRINT SCALE: It's important to use a large number of prints to achieve a visual sensation of motion. You should have a wide variety of print scales and types, ranging from solids and tiny prints to widely spaced prints and large prints including florals and paisleys, and even tight geometrics (which I call *men's underwear prints*—what you would expect to see on vintage boxer shorts from the Goodwill or thrift store).

You can determine whether a fabric is a large-scale print by cutting a 2″ square or a hole the size of a 50-cent piece in a piece of paper and moving the 2″ opening over the surface of the fabric. If you are viewing a large-scale print of pink flowers and green leaves on a black background, the fabric you can see through the 2″ opening may occasionally be completely pink or completely green, or completely black.

Large-scale prints will also act as *walking* or *talking* fabrics, serving as a transition between fabrics of different colors. The pink and green, black-background floral print, for example, could serve as a transition fabric between blacks and pinks, or pinks and greens, and so on.

Several large-scale prints used together create a lot of movement from one area of your design to another. They are especially useful for blurring the eye and creating incredible visual effects. It becomes impossible for the eye to tell when it travels from the black area and moves into the pinks. It's a pleasant sensation to end up somewhere and not remember the specifics of the journey! You can also use value changes and color migration to make transitions between groups of fabrics.

A medium-scale print will have different areas of color or value viewed through an opening 1″ square or the size of a quarter. Small-scale prints do not appear to change from one area to the next, even if viewed through an opening of only ½″ or the size of a dime.

COLOR GROUPS: If you have two color groups that are similar, add one or two fabrics that further define each color. For example, if you have a group of **blue**-greens and a group of **green**-blues, add a distinct blue fabric to the blue-greens and a distinct green fabric to the green-blues. This adds visual distinction and interest, which keeps the eye moving and thus the brain entertained!

Flirting fabrics are also fun to create. Flirting fabrics are fabrics which show off another color within them that is either: a) not in the quilt at all, or b) not a color in that area of the strata. Thus the fabric is flirting rather than fully expressed. It is a delightful effect. They flirt with objects of common color in the room or with a different area of the quilt.

ISOLATED FABRICS: If a fabric stands out, it needs a friend. Add one or two similar fabrics. Never eliminate a fabric because it stands out; always add a similar fabric to create an accent area and richness. The added fabric(s) can be similar in color, value, or print type; match whichever characteristic necessary to give the odd fabric a friend.

When you are happy with your group of fabrics, you are ready to arrange them in the order they will appear in your Bargello Tapestry design. This is discussed in the next chapter, **Strata Planning**.

A FINAL NOTE

Every quilter loves fabric. We are passionate about combining many fabrics because we are exciting and excitable people and our hearts and emotions are involved. If we allow ourselves to become concerned and anxious about the "correct" use of fabrics, we restrict and thus defeat our creative and artistic birthright. Thinking that we could do it "wrong" interferes with our attraction to fabric in general. If fear and inhibition surface, they paralyze our ability to think and act freely. When you use these guidelines, do so with confidence. They will assure you of a spectacular and visually rich Bargello Tapestry quilt every time. Don't let your intellect downgrade your heart!

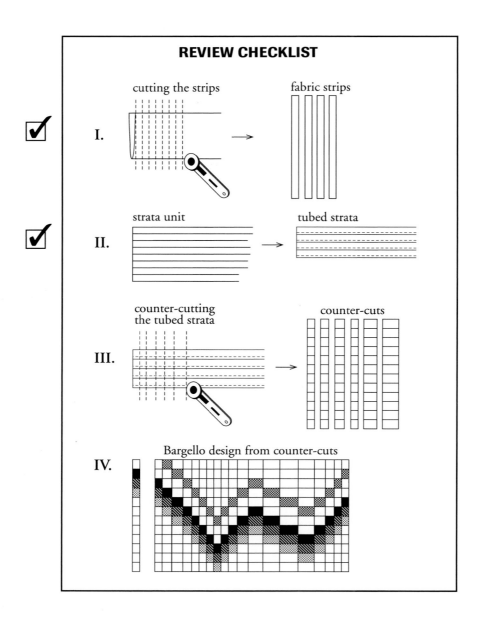

REVIEW CHECKLIST

I. cutting the strips → fabric strips

II. strata unit → tubed strata

III. counter-cutting the tubed strata → counter-cuts

IV. Bargello design from counter-cuts

CHAPTER   6

STRATA PLANNING:
CLOSE-CONTRAST FABRIC ARRANGEMENT

You have read the chapter on fabric selection and have your 30 fabrics. Now they need to be arranged into the order they will have in the strata. Close-contrast blending between values and colors is the key to sensational and dramatic effects.

First of all, a word of warning: *strata is nothing to look at*—in fact, it is unattractive. Unless you have a great deal of familiarity with strata creation and use, it will shake your confidence to see beautiful fabrics arranged and sewn together this way. It is impossible to imagine the transformation that will occur later when the strata are used to create a Bargello Tapestry pattern. You cannot possibly see what the Bargello Tapestry quilt will look like at this early stage. Just follow the close-contrast guidelines and relax about the outcome. I assure you it will be dazzling!

NOTE TO TEACHERS: If you intend to teach Bargello Tapestry quiltmaking, always reserve some strata from each of your quilts. It is an invaluable and essential teaching aid. When students see your homely strata and then the transformation into an exquisite Bargello Tapestry design, they will be less anxious about their own beautiful fabrics appearing homely at the strata level.

CLOSE-CONTRAST: DEFINITION

I call my blending and blurring method of fabric arrangement *close-contrast*. In close-contrast, fabrics are arranged by similarities. They can be similar in color, value, and/or print scale so that they visually blur or flow from one to another. Groups of fabrics are then combined into *runs* from lightest to darkest, and then several of these runs are joined together to create the whole strata unit or sequence.

Within each run there should be a visually smooth flow from the lighter to the darker fabrics. Your eye should not stop or rest on any single fabric. The run should not have flat or muddy areas; there should be a constant progression from the lighter to the darker fabrics though the print scales and colors.

As you go from light to medium to dark be sure to include

multicolored fabrics and a range of print scales. Include unexpected colors to join forces here and there—don't forget the 10% risk factor. Let the blues get a bit purple, the reds a bit brown, the greens a little aqua (or even yellow), and the oranges a bit red.

If viewed at a distance of about 10 feet, the fabrics should lose their individual voices and work into a rich unified expression. By creating several individual runs of close-contrast fabrics and then playing with these runs, positioning them to flow into one another by joining the light and dark areas of two runs, you create effects I call *hills, valleys,* and *cliffs.* The strata then becomes a unit of motion, with each run flowing into the next. Colors, values, and print textures ebb and flow, swell and recede. This overall sensation of fabrics acting like a single unit, swelling and receding, creates a visual illusion of tremendous, cohesive depth in the final quilt.

As you read through this chapter about close-contrast, look carefully at the photographed quilts. Inspect the fabric selections and the arrangements for the use of close-contrast effects. These quilts, offered to you as a collection, show you the diversity that can be achieved by using close-contrast techniques to create sensational effects. As you examine the quilts you will begin to sense intuitively how to create close-contrast effects yourself. There are always many options and avenues for creative license. *Any group of close-contrast fabrics could be arranged in numerous ways, all of which would be wonderful.* Relax, allow your creativity to flow as well as your fabrics!

BUILDING FABRIC RUNS

An individual fabric run includes all three values: light, medium, and dark. The values progress in a smooth transition from light to dark or dark to light. The colors can be from a single color family or they can be numerous unrelated colors. *Value* is the issue, not color. Short, medium and long runs simply have a different number of fabrics in the light to dark sequence (Figures 6-1A & 6-1B).

■ Sort your fabrics into color groups

To begin, sort your fabrics into general color groups. Work quickly; go with your first impression of each fabric. If it has more than one color, do not ponder and inspect it, just decide quickly based on your first impression. If an individual fabric reads purple, it goes in the purple group. If it reads "kind of purple" it also goes into the purple group. If it reads rather blue and there is no blue category, then it goes in (you guessed it) the purple group!

Blue, purple, black, and even maroon can appear very similar when viewed together from a distance of 10 feet. A broad range of colors creating a group adds richness; an assortment of fabric colors that are not perfectly coordinated is refreshing and adventuresome. Unexpected

Figure 6-1A
Fabric Texture Gradations

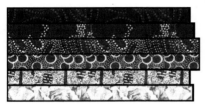

Figure 6-1B
A. Long run

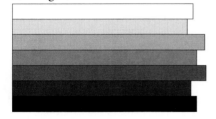

B. Medium run

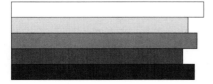

C. Short run

combinations add visual character to your quilt; people will stop and study your work. They will think you have a profound sense of color and a masterful control over fabrics. They will believe that you always knew what you were doing! They will admire your confidence and artistry. So . . . take a risk, stretch your color sense a little. Your enrichment will encourage others to do so as well.

■ Arrange the fabrics in each color group by value

Start with the lightest and work your way through the mediums to the darks. Remember, the value of any fabric is relative to the fabrics around it. When compared to black (the darkest value), and white (the lightest value), all other fabrics look medium—medium dark, medium light, and so on. If you have no extremely dark or light fabrics in your group, then medium fabrics will step forward and function as dark and light candidates.

It often helps to squint your eyes and evaluate only two fabrics at a time. When you compare only two fabrics at a time: the lighter value will appear to advance, the darker value will appear to recede. Some people find it helpful to lay a piece of white fabric and a piece of black fabric at the beginning and the end of the fabric sequence to determine those fabrics closer to white or closer to black. These ideas should help you arrange your fabrics in a light to medium to dark sequence; then remove the white and black fabrics and *voilà*, your fabric run has been determined.

Sometimes our acceptance of a color predesignates its value. For instance, yellow–orange–red is often considered a light–medium–dark sequence by color family. Yet cream–yellow–brown can also be considered a light–medium–dark value sequence by color family. Other examples are: 1) white–pink–red; 2) pink–red–black; 3) yellow–brown–black;
4) lavender–purple–maroon; you may find these more interesting than light green–medium green–dark green, which is very obvious.

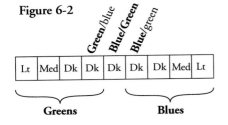

Figure 6-2

■ Combine different color groups in the same run

Don't restrict yourself to one color group per run. There can be color migration in a run from one color family to another, using multicolored fabrics (walking or talking fabrics) to make the transition, as long as the dark to light value gradation is maintained (Figure 6-2).

You might also choose to disregard color entirely within a run and order the fabrics by value or print scale only, resulting in a colorful and beautiful scrappy effect with no impression of a specific color development, only light to dark.

Figure 6-3

A. Dark background, small light dots

B. Dark background, medium light dots

C. Dark background, large light dots

■ Include areas where value is determined by print scale

Value can be due to print scale as well as color. Imagine a design of white polka-dots on a black background. What value do you think of? It could be light or dark depending on the size of the dots *and* the space between the dots. A fabric with a black background and small, widely scattered white dots will appear very dark. The larger and closer together the dots, the lighter the fabric appears (Figure 6-3, A, B, & C).

A fabric with a black background might not be treated as a dark. For example, a value run between white and black could use grey for the medium value or a black-and-white print could be used, in which case the medium value is a black-and-white print, not a grey. Figure 6-4 has several black and white prints used as medium values.

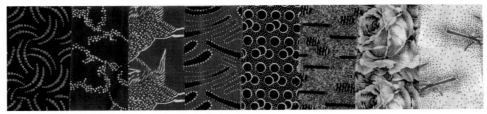

Figure 6-4

Figure 6-5

A. Light: Navy/White

B. Medium: Navy/White

C. Dark: Navy/White

D. Very dark: Navy/White

■ Include lacy areas

A series of prints which are similar, but gradually run from light to dark, can be used to create what I call *lacy* areas in your strata. Several of these fabrics placed side by side in your strata will produce an area that from a distance looks like lace because of the visual movement they encourage as the density of print scale changes from widely spaced to very compact. Usually, lacy effects are created with fabrics that have similar colors expressed (Figure 6-5, A, B, C, & D).

■ Use long and short runs to make thick and thin areas in the strata plan

The length of a run, meaning how many fabrics are included in it, will create different effects in your strata and thus in your Bargello Tapestry quilt. There are thick, medium, and thin runs, and they create larger and smaller undulations in the overall strata composition.

A run of only three or four fabrics makes a *thin* area in the strata plan. You eye enters and exits quickly, like a quick accent or pulse.

Five to nine fabrics make a *medium* run, somewhere between thin and thick runs in appearance and effect.

A run of 10 or more fabrics makes a *thick* area in the strata plan. A thick run is a restful, lazy, "get-lost-in-it" area, and your eye takes longer to absorb it. Contrasting values that undulate create the sensations of depth in your quilt.

■ Use difficult fabrics as "walking" fabrics

"Spotty" fabrics can be difficult to assign a specific value to. They usually have dark and light areas, such as dark figures on a light background, light figures on a dark background, pink flowers on a black background, and so on. Consider them to be medium values, not dark or light. If from 10 feet back they do not fit in your value run as mediums, they can be used to create great transitional movement from one run to another. I call these "walking" or "talking" fabrics, because they have more than one voice and can form a bridge between two dissimilar fabrics or two runs.

Other fabrics will defy your attempts to place them in a single value category because two or more distinct values are present. Large-scale prints usually include very different values. These fabrics must be considered medium values. They can create wonderful, tingling, dancing areas when several of them are placed side by side. They can also be used as transitional fabrics between color groups. These are fabrics I call *talking* or *walking* fabrics.

■ Add similar fabrics near any one fabric that stands out

As you are creating runs, always watch for individual fabrics that stand out too much. If one fabric is especially obvious, it needs to have several similar pieces added as friends. These fabric friends dilute whatever the obvious area is and blend it effectively. This will blur the questionable fabric so that it moves with the rest of the run, acting like a spicy accent rather than an obnoxious individual. If you really wish to feature an individual fabric, consider using the fabric as a spacer section. See Chapter 10, **Bargello Pattern Flow.**

■ Examine your fabrics by the light of the moon . . .

I once viewed my king-size Amish quilt on the wall of an upstairs hallway beneath moonlit skylights at 3:30 in the morning. The quilt looked so different than it did in daylight, it stopped me in my tracks. Certain areas glowed and others completely disappeared. Ever since, I have enjoyed viewing my fabric arrangements by moonlight. (Being a night owl helps!) This particular quilt had 13 fabrics in five different runs of five to seven fabrics per run, in a light-dark, light-dark, light-dark and so on cliff pattern. The lights of every run were up against the darks of the next run. This contrast encouraged the visual glow I saw in the moonlight.

Lay your fabrics edge to edge, with about 2″ of each showing and no spaces between. Stand several feet away by the light switch and look at the fabric assortment as a whole. Continue to look at the fabrics as you switch the light off, and note the value differences your eyes perceive in moonlight. Turn the light back on to see the original effect. Repeat until you are wiser and no longer entertained!

STRATA COMPOSITION

Sequential, Repeat and Reverse Repeat

Each strata unit when complete has a fabric composition that is one of three types. The entire sequence of cloth from the first to the last strip can be: 1) *sequential,* 2) *repeat,* 3) *reverse-repeat.*

These three overall styles can be created with any number of fabrics and incorporating any number of arrangements of runs. In a *sequential* arrangement the entire composition, whatever it is, occurs one time only. A *repeat* strata has a sequential composition appearing at least two times in an exact repeat of itself, start to finish. A *reverse-repeat* has a sequential composition appearing at least two times, *but* in a reverse order every other time that it is used.

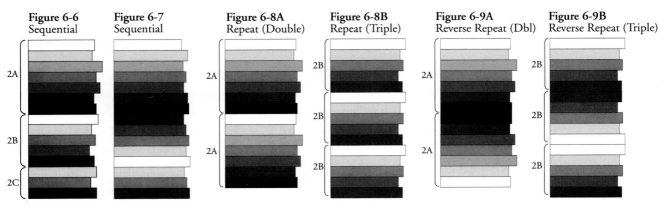

Figure 6-6
Sequential

Figure 6-7
Sequential

Figure 6-8A
Repeat (Double)

Figure 6-8B
Repeat (Triple)

Figure 6-9A
Reverse Repeat (Dbl)

Figure 6-9B
Reverse Repeat (Triple)

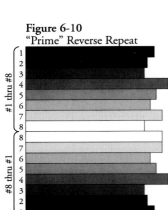

Figure 6-10
"Prime" Reverse Repeat

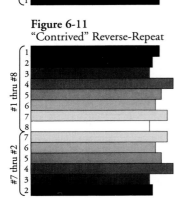

Figure 6-11
"Contrived" Reverse-Repeat

In a sequential series, each of the fabrics is used only once in the strata. Using 15 fabrics, the fabrics could be ordered 1 through 15 and none would be repeated. You can have any number of runs within the 15 fabrics (Figures 6-6 & 6-7). Both show three runs.

If you want to have a *repeat* in your strata, for a 14 strip strata unit you would select 7 fabrics that would run 1 through 7, then 1 through 7 again (Figure 6-8A) Figure 6-8B shows a triple repeat of 5 fabrics creating 15 fabric positions.

It is also possible to arrange the fabrics so you have a *reverse-repeat* fabric flow (Figures 6-9A) (Figure 6-9B shows triple).

In a *prime reverse-repeat* the entire fabric sequence of the run is repeated; the fabrics would run 1 through 8, then 8 through 1(Figure 6-10), having 16 fabric positions. Prime reverse-repeats are visually powerful because they strengthen the effect of the first and last fabrics as they *double-up*—a double-up being where there are two strips of an identical fabric side by side in the strata. They create an effect similar to a small River Spacer (see **Spacer Section**, page 30).

In a *contrived reverse-repeat*, the fabrics are reversed and repeated without a double-up. A contrived reverse-repeat would be 1 through 8, then 7 through 2; a total of 14 strips. When you tube the strata, fabric 2 would sew to fabric 1, completing the repeat and creating a perfect flow with no double ups (Figure 6-11).

NOTE: Figures for repeat and reverse show one run only for simplicity. However, *any sequence* using any number of individual runs can be repeated or reverse repeated in its entirety.

Look through the quilts in this book and try to find examples of quilts that use the repeat, reverse-repeat, and sequential strata plans. Then check your assessment by reading through the summary listed with each quilt in **Appendix B** to see if your assessment is on track. (Actual strata compositions are detailed for every quilt in Appendix B.) Note your reaction to each to understand your own individual preferences. NOTE: Read the section on Spacers (page 30) to understand the additional effects that can be created. It is possible to use a River spacer, an Island spacer, or a Background spacer with any of the three fabric arrangements: repeat, reverse-repeat, and sequential—a total of nine different combinations!

Combining Fabric Runs

Arrange your fabrics into several runs, each based on color, value, and print scale or a combination of all three (Figure 6-12). A Bargello Tapestry quilt in which several runs are combined is much more complex and pleasing than one which has only one run, or runs of equal numbers. The effect of depth is rich and sophisticated, with great visual character.

Figure 6-12
A. Long run   B. Medium run   C. Short run

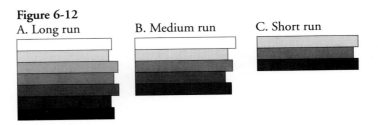

Combining Runs for Depth and Illusions

Figure 6-13A   6-13B   6-13C
Hills and Valleys

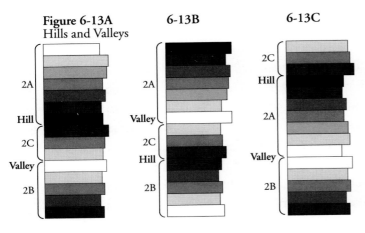

■ **Hills, valleys, and cliffs**

The transition between two runs can be obvious and abrupt, or mysterious and gradual. Both methods are attractive and effective. I call the gradual transitions *hills and valleys* and the abrupt ones *cliffs.*

Hill: When the darks of one run merge with the darks of another run, a *hill* is formed. If the darks are very dark or numerous, then the hill is more like a mountain. If the darks tend toward medium or involve fewer fabrics, then the hill is more shallow. Both are fine and good, and it is

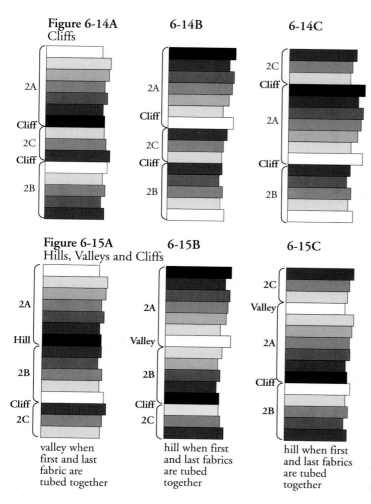

Figure 6-14A
Cliffs

6-14B

6-14C

Figure 6-15A
Hills, Valleys and Cliffs

6-15B

6-15C

valley when first and last fabric are tubed together

hill when first and last fabrics are tubed together

hill when first and last fabrics are tubed together

desirable to have some of each in the same strata plan. The contrast between values creates the depth that is so intriguing (Figures 6-13A, B, C). A design lacking this depth can look pasty and flat.

Valley: When the lights of one run merge with the lights of another run, a *valley* is formed. If the lights are very light or numerous, then the valley is deep and wide. If the lights tend toward medium or involve fewer fabrics, then the valley is more shallow. Again, both are fine and good and you should try to include both.

Cliff: If the lights of one run are joined to the darks of another run, a *cliff* is formed. This is an abrupt awakening to the eye. There is a sharp, distinct, single line where two fabrics meet. On either side of the clash there are close-contrast fabrics that build up each run (Fig. 6-14A, B, C). A cliff is a refreshing accent in the Bargello Tapestry quilt. It creates the illusion of instant depth. Use cliffs sparingly and space them apart. They should emphasize the rolling waves of your Bargello Tapestry design, not chop them up into little pieces.

CAUTION: Only one edge of each fabric should be involved in the cliff effect. Seeing one seam where two fabrics join is acceptable. Seeing both seams of one fabric creates a stripe of the fabric that is not desirable—like a dancer that deliberately dominates a chorus line. Individual fabrics should not stand out unless they are *spacer* fabrics which stand out by sheer volume, not necessarily by color or value contrast.

■ Using transitional fabrics between runs

Walking or talking fabrics are large-scale prints with two or three dominant colors. They "walk" between two different color groups or values and blur them together. Walkers allow you to put two different groups together with no jarring break in between. If you aren't satisfied with an area where two runs merge, try adding some walking fabrics at that location. A walker between a green run and a red run could be a green-and-red print of whatever value is appropriate. Walkers make the transition between two groups subtle and mysterious. The more walkers, the more mystery!!

Spacer Section

A spacer section is an extra wide strip of fabric sewn between two of the regular strips in the strata plan. The width of the spacer strip makes a dramatic difference in the Bargello Tapestry quilt. The spacer can be anywhere in the strata plan. The illustrations show the spacers on the edge for simplicity and for clarity of proportions.

■ River spacer

A River spacer is only moderately wide and gently influences the Bargello design (Figure 6-16). It will have the look of a thick river of fabric flowing within and around the Bargello pattern. It does not dramatically alter the effect or motion of the overall design. A River spacer is always less than one-half of the total combined height of the individual strips in the strata unit. For example, if the strata height is 30″, the river spacer can be up to 15″. In this example, the maximum (total) strata height would be 45″. The spacer is part of the tubed strata unit and can be placed anywhere among the strata strips.

■ Background spacer

A Background spacer is very large and very dramatic, and completely changes the Bargello design (Figure 6-17). The Background spacer fabric stays at the top and bottom of the Bargello design, completely surrounding the active movement. The Bargello design appears to float on the Background spacer which extends above and below it; hence the term, Background spacer. The cut width of a Background spacer is always equal to or larger than the combined height of the individual strips in the strata unit. For example, if the strata height is 30″, the background spacer can be up 30″ or more. In this example, the minimum (total) strata height would be 60″. The spacer is part of the tubed strata unit.

■ Island spacer

An Island spacer creates islands of Bargello designs (Figure 6-18). Its effect is a cross between both a River spacer and a Background spacer. It will look like a Background spacer that decided not to stay completely in the background, unable to contain the sweeping movement of the Bargello design. It will also appear to be a very wide river, creating floating islands of Bargello activity. An Island spacer is from half to all of the combined height of the individual strips in the strata unit. For example, if the strata height is 30″, the island spacer can be from 15″ up to 30″. The overall strata height would then be from 45″–60″.

Look for each of these spacer effects in the color photographs and check your assessment by reading about the strata style used. This information is below each quilt and fully identified in Appendix B.

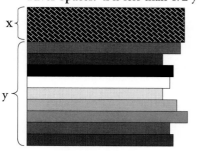

Figure 6-16
River Spacer: x is less than 1/2 y

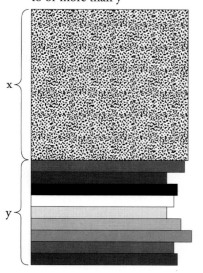

Figure 6-17
Background Spacer: x is equal to or more than y

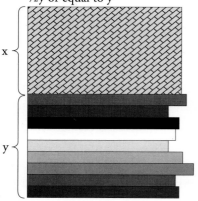

Figure 6-18
Island Spacer: x is between ½y or equal to y

EVALUATING YOUR STRATA PLAN

Checkpoint A

When you have your individual runs organized into a flow, step back and look at the overall effect from a distance. Remember you are not looking for pretty, you are looking for flow. Do the values in each run flow smoothly from light to dark? If the values seem to stair-step jarringly, add a fabric or two of the missing values. Are all the runs similar in length? This can be boring. Add fabrics to some runs and remove fabrics from others to create an unequal pulse over the entire sequence.

Does the overall strata plan have at least some areas of light, medium, and dark? The overall value of the quilt can be very light with just a hint of a darkish area, or very darkish with just a few light, glowing fabrics, but be sure you include the whole range of values in order to create the illusion of depth in the final Bargello Tapestry quilt.

Remember, strata is usually not attractive. Close-contrast fabric arrangement is a very different approach to fabric arrangement. Evaluate your arrangement for blur. No one fabric should jump out, no matter how much you like it. Don't place fabrics side by side just because you think they look pretty together.

Checkpoint B

Last of all, remember that your strata is not going to be seen as a unit of strips, top to bottom, but as a continuous series with no top and bottom; almost as if someone finger-painted with the strata to blur and blend it. Does the first fabric in your strata blur with the last fabric? These two fabrics, the first and last, will touch as often as any other fabrics in your quilt. Add additional fabrics or rearrange the existing ones as necessary to make the first and last fabrics merge as gracefully as the rest.

Don't move fabrics around just because you think your overall plan isn't pretty. Most strata plans are quite homely; you can't see their real beauty until they are cut up and moved around into the flowing waves of a Bargello Tapestry design. Also, don't continue to alter an arrangement looking for the "right" order. If you have wonderful light, medium, and dark fabrics, lots of close-contrast similarities, and several walking fabrics, there are literally twenty or more great arrangements possible with the same fabrics. None is the "right" one, and none is better than the others. They all use the same fabrics, just differently. Make a choice and get on to the cutting and sewing and counter-cutting!

With so many fabrics to choose from and so many different strata plans to create, one Bargello quilt can never satisfy all of your creativity. Make a choice and go forward.

STRATA CONSTRUCTION

The strata unit is the basic "dough" of every Bargello quilt. Individual strips of three or more fabrics are sewn together along their long edges to begin. Strata units for Bargello Tapestry quilts are primarily made of strips cut the same width. In all of the calculations in this book, the strips are assumed to be cut from 45"-wide fabric. Most quilters cut these strips selvedge to selvedge, perpendicular to the fold in the fabric as it comes off the bolt. The strips will actually be 40"–46" long. Any 40"–46"-wide fabric will yield adequately for these Bargello style quilts and the yardage charts provided in Chapter 12.

You may cut the strips parallel to the selvedges if you prefer. Some fabrics are stronger cut parallel to the selvedges; you might also prefer to cut strips this way to take advantage of a printed stripe, or if you are working with a vintage fabric only 36" wide. If you wish to cut parallel to the selvedge you must either purchase at least 1¼ yards of fabric, or splice your fabric as often as necessary so you can create strips that are 45" long.

The total amount of fabric needed for your strata unit depends upon several factors: how wide each strip is and how many strips are used, the style of your design (repeat, reverse-repeat, sequential, and so on), and the final desired height and width of your quilt. Yardage calculations are extensively covered in Chapter 12 on **Strata Math** for *each* consideration.

SEWING THE STRATA UNIT

It is very important to sew the individual fabric strips together with as little distortion as possible when creating the strata unit. *A stitch in time saves nine*—no one likes to remove seams. (I call this reverse sewing!)

Distortion can originate from any number of sources—poor cloth, poor machine adjustment, or poor handling of the fabrics while sewing, cutting, and/or ironing. Follow these guidelines:

1. Carefully keep the long edges of the two strips aligned evenly at the raw edges while sewing the entire length of the seam.
2. Start the ends of the strips even but don't try to match the other ends; strips cut from different fabrics will not be exactly the same length.

3. Always stitch from the same (beginning) end of the strata unit, toward the opposite (leftover) end of the strips. **Do not sew up one edge and down the opposite edge.**

4. For strata with numerous strips, sew together six to seven strips at a time, then join these subunits together to avoid damage from overhandling.

5. Don't force or pull the strips as they feed through the sewing machine. Pinning is fine if you prefer it, but it isn't necessary if you can keep the strips aligned without overhandling them.

6. Keep your stitch length constant over the length of the seam.

7. Use the same seam width in each seam in the strata unit.

8. Use the same sewing machine for identical strata units

> NOTE: It is easier to maintain a constant seam width if you use the same sewing machine for all the strata units for one quilt, and if you sew all the seams with the same light source so the shadows are always the same. A different machine can safely be used to sew the quilt together *after* the counter-cutting of the strata.

ALERT! THINGS NOT TO DO

Do not pull on the strips at all. As you sew two strips together:

1. Do NOT pull the top strip toward you.
2. Do NOT pull the bottom strip toward you.
3. Do NOT pull both strips toward you or both strips away from you from behind the needle.
4. Do NOT pull both strips toward you as you simultaneously pull both strips away from you from the back side of the needle. Fabric stretches easily when it is in strips.

If you follow these directions and distortion still develops, it can be traced to one of several sources:

1. Poorly cut strips—either not straight, or not identical. See **Rotary Cutting Tools and Techniques**, Chapter 3.

2. Problems with your sewing machine—dull needle, improper throat plate, improper feed-dog pressure, poor quality thread or too large a spool.

   a) Try replacing your needle. Consult your sewing machine manual. Take your machine in for maintenance and explain the problem. Buy a new machine—call it your "good girl" gift.

   b) Put large spools of thread in a Mason jar behind the sewing machine so that the thread is under no tension as it feeds off the spool.

3. Problems with your ironing technique. See **Ironing Strata**, below.

4. Poor fabric quality—loosely woven cotton, polyester, rayon, metallics, and so on. Use premium 100% cotton fabric intended for quiltmaking. Try to "beef up" troublesome fabrics before cutting the strips with spray starch, or iron fusible webbing to the wrong

Figure 7-1

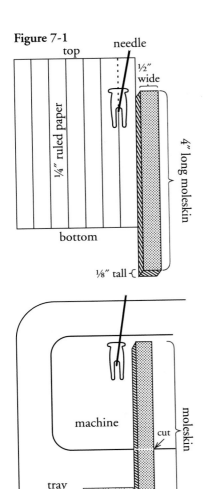

side of the fabric.

SEWING ACCURATE 1/4″ SEAMS

To help you make consistent ¼″ seams, make a wall guide that extends 4″ from the sewing machine needle toward you and ¼″ to the right of the needle. Follow instructions A and B to create a wall guide.

(A) Trim a piece of ¼″ gridded graph paper or ¼″ ruled paper exactly on one of the lines. Stitch on a line ¼″ in from the edge for about 2″ to correctly align the paper under the presser foot.

(B) Purchase a package of Dr. Scholl's Moleskin™ and cut a thin strip ½″ wide and 4″ long. Remove the paper backing from the strip to expose the sticky back. Using the paper edge (as shown) for your guide, place the moleskin on the throat plate of your machine. (If there is a tray on your machine that must be removed for bobbin winding, *have it in place as you position the moleskin*, but then slice through the strip with a razor blade so the tray can be removed.) There will be a portion of moleskin on each unit of the sewing machne (Figure 7-1).

When you sew strips together, align them and then feed them through exactly at the wall formed by the edge of the moleskin. This will keep your eyes away from the needle and reduce eyestrain. You will sew a consistent ¼″ seam with amazing speed and ease.

NOTE: For Bargello style quilts, a *consistent seam width* is important, no matter what width is used.

IRONING STRATA

It is essential to iron all the seams in every strata unit before any counter-cutting occurs. Since heat and steam can dramatically effect cloth, it is esssential to follow the procedures outlined below to minimize distortion. If the ironing process is mishandled, it will be difficult to accurately counter-cut and counter-sew the Bargello design. Improper ironing can cause distortions.

1. **All of the seams in one strata unit should travel in one direction**: either up toward the first strip or down toward the last strip.
2. Of the total number of strata units constructed for your quilt, **half should have their seams ironed up and half should have their seams ironed down** (Figure 7-2A). If there are four strata units

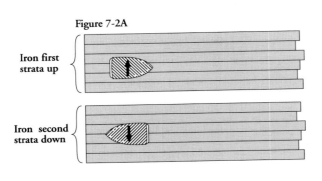

Figure 7-2A

Iron first strata up

Iron second strata down

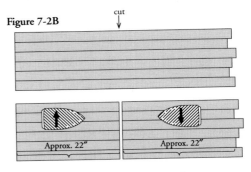

Figure 7-2B

Approx. 22″   Approx. 22″

required, iron two up and two down. With an odd number of strata units (1, 3, 5, etc.), cut one in half crosswise so that one strata unit is in two pieces, each about 22″ long, then iron one of these up and the other one down (Fig. 7-2B).

The reason to iron half the seams up and half the seams down is to reduce the bulk when sewing the counter-cuts together and create perfect seam intersections. Counter-cuts are made from both strata tubes during the creation of the design. They are cut alternately from one tube, then the other. Thus one counter-cut will have "up" seams and the next counter-cut will have "down" seams. The seam allowances will "avoid" one another naturally (Figure 7-3).

Figure 7-3

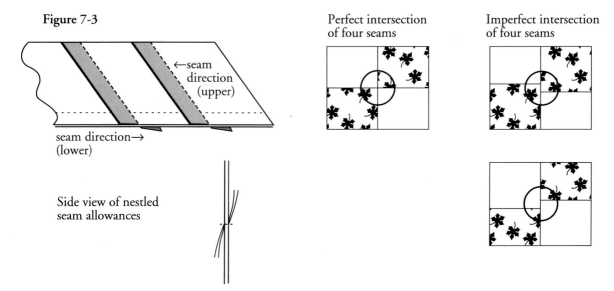

←seam direction (upper)

seam direction→ (lower)

Side view of nestled seam allowances

Perfect intersection of four seams

Imperfect intersection of four seams

FOLLOW THESE STEPS TO PERFECT IRONING

To iron the unit accurately and effectively you must use heat and steam. The position of the strata unit on the ironing board is also critical. You must place the strata unit so you are ironing *across the seams* rather than lengthwise along the seams (Figure 7-4).

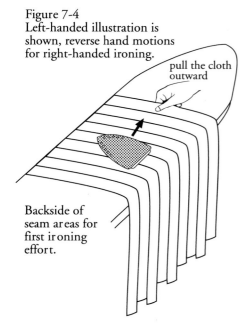

Figure 7-4
Left-handed illustration is shown, reverse hand motions for right-handed ironing.

pull the cloth outward

Backside of seam areas for first ironing effort.

1. Place the strata unit wrong side up *across* the ironing board, not along the length of the board.
2. Begin ironing edge-to-edge in the middle of the strata unit and then gradually work toward one end. Then go back to the middle and work toward the other end.
3. With your free hand, grasp one edge of the strata unit and pull the cloth outward as the iron goes across the seams. This will expose the full width of each strip and eliminate accordian pleating.
4. Use the broad side of the iron, not the point.
5. Push the iron in one direction only, toward your free hand, then pick it up and repeat the motion, always from the same edge.
6. Do not push the iron back and forth.

7. Use the hot cotton setting *with steam.* Steam is your friend! It will help block the strata and flatten the seam allowances.

After you have ironed the whole strata unit from the wrong side, turn it over and repeat the ironing process from the right side. Check each strip on the right side for an even, consistent width exposure. The strata unit should lie very flat when viewed from the right side of the fabrics; it should not puff up at all.

After ironing the strata unit from the front side, check to make sure the seam allowances are still flat and uncreased on the wrong side. If they stick up they will act like little feet when you place your ruler on the strata unit to make a counter-cut; the little feet will smash down and walk, distorting the seams of the strata unit as you make counter-cuts. This is not desirable.

After ironing, inspect the wrong side of the strata unit. All seam allowances should lie flat and smooth:

(a) they should not stand up away from the strata unit

(b) they should not have any creases.

After ironing, a visual check on the right side should show all strips to be equally wide, and they should be the same width for their entire length. There should be no *accordian pleating,* false creases near the seams. *A perfect strata should lie flat—there should be no puffiness, waves, arches, lettuce leaves, or rainbows. If these exist, go to "Check and Correct."* Don't worry, there are solutions.

CHECK AND CORRECT

After the strata has been created—i.e., cut, sewn, and ironed—it must be checked for irregularities. All necessary corrections must be made before it can be tubed and counter-cut. If there are problems in the strata unit—due to fabric selection, arrangement, cutting, sewing, or ironing—and you continue through the counter-cutting procedures, you will be multiplying your problems. Often, a few of the long straight seams need minor adjustments. *If you bypass the check and correct procedure, you will be adjusting and fussing with hundreds of smaller seams later.* It's not a pleasant experience, rather like being in 4th gear on the freeway and throwing the transmission into reverse.

NOTE: Keep in mind that even if it is necessary to correct something, these strata-based techniques are very fast. So breathe easy and take your time. Always go forward with accuracy; don't be quick to cut up mistakes, you'll just get *lots* of little mistakes!

■ Perfect Strata

When your quilt requires several strata units it is essential that they be identical. Each must have:

(a) the same number of strips

Figure 7-5A Perfect parallel

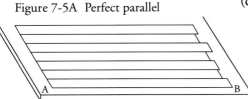

Figure 7-5B Distortion "Rainbow arch"

Figure 7-5C
Seam too delicate

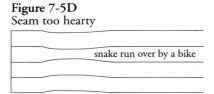

snake swallowed a mouse

Figure 7-5D
Seam too hearty

snake run over by a bike

Figure 7-6

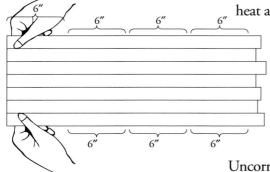

(b) sewn in the same order, and

(c) each strata unit must have identical seam allowances.

(d) If the seam allowances are all the same, each strata unit should be the same height.

Compare the height at the end of one unit to the end of another. Then compare the middle heights from one to another. **Do not compare ends to middles, as there can be a ¼″ to ½″ difference even in the same strata unit.** These differences are due to the extra thickness and density of the selvedges at the ends and our tendency to stitch differently at the ends than in the middle of the strips. **If ends match ends and middles match middles nothing needs adjusting.**

After ironing your strata units and checking them against each other, spread each out as flat and smooth as it will naturally lay. Line up the beginning and ending edge of the last fabric with the long edge of a table from points A to B (Figure 7-5A).

(e) If your strata unit lies wonderfully straight and flat (Figure 7-5A), skip to **Tubing the Strata**, Chapter 8.

(f) If it does not, your strata has a problem and it needs to be checked and corrected. Figure 7-5B has a rainbow, Figures 7-5 C&D have snake channels. Try to locate your problem in the illustrations that follow and read the text for the solution to each condition.

UNEQUAL STRATA HEIGHTS

■ Accordion pleating

The strata unit may have areas which are not ironed out completely to their fullest sewn width. You may not be able to see the accordian pleats until you pull the strata unit gently edge to edge (not end to end) to expose them. Check every 6″ along the entire length of the strata unit (Figure 7-6).

Accordian pleats are sneaky, but once you discover them they are easy to correct. You need to re-iron the strata unit more aggressively and with heat and steam. Go back and read through the section on ironing strata. With the weight of the iron holding the unit down on one side, pull the strata in the other direction with your free hand. Expose the pleats and iron each strip as broad and flat and wide as it was sewn.

Uncorrected accordian pleats will cause numerous problems, all of which take away from the accuracy and speed of making the quilt, and add to your fussing and fuming. Uncorrected, they will cause inaccurate counter-sewing and irregular seam junctions, inaccurate and irregular quilt size, and a puffy and distorted quilt surface.

■ Cutting and sewing errors

If there is more than a ½″ difference between the height of two different strata units, check for one or more strips that are clearly a different width. If you find one, check to see if your seam width was off, or if you cut the strip too wide or two narrow. When you find a strip width that is off, correct it before you check the rest of the strips. One non-uniform strip can set off a domino reaction that kicks everything after the problem area out of whack as well. Repairing one strip may bring all the others back in line.

HOW TO CORRECT THE PROBLEM — 4 SOLUTIONS

1. If a strip was cut too wide, remove one seam. Recut the strip to the proper size, then resew it into the strata.
2. If a strip was cut too narrow, then either replace the strip with one cut the proper width, or remove both of the seams in that strip and resew, taking less than a ¼″ seam from the narrow strip only. **Be sure to take a normal ¼″ seam from the two neighboring strips that** *were* **properly cut.**

OPTION: Don't correct anything. Use half-staggers (Figure 7-7) or vertical interruptions (Figure 7-8) when sewing the counter-cuts together. With either of these techniques the seam junctions are not matched, so any irregularities will not be visible. The effects are beautiful and the technique can be a good solution to the problem of irregular strata rather than redoing any efforts or feeling bad about yourself. Review the photos showing these features. Gallery quilts 19 and 29 each used half-staggered. Chapter 9 shows the cutting techniques for half staggers (see Figure 9-5), and Chapter 10 discusses vertical interruptions (see Figure 10-12)■

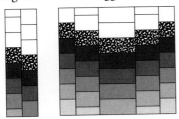

Figure 7-7 Half-staggers

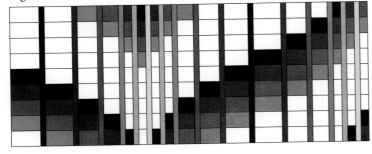

Figure 7-8 Vertical interruptions

Figure 7-9A
Seam too delicate

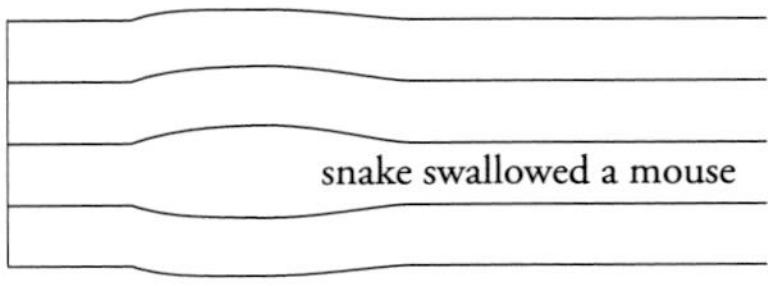

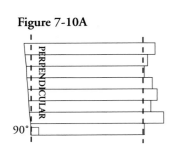

snake swallowed a mouse

Figure 7-9B
Seam too hearty

snake run over by a bike

Figure 7-10A

PERPENDICULAR

90°

SNAKES!–Irregular seams

Sometimes your seam width varies within the length of one seam, usually due to moving your wrist slightly. If you stitch hearty or shy of a perfect ¼″ seam, the exposed fabric strip will be altered. It can be narrower and will look like a snake that has been slightly flattened by a bicycle tire or wider causing the exposed strip to look like a snake that has swallowed a small mouse. Both situations require correction (Figures 7-9A & 7-9B).

To correct thin snake channels remove the length of the seam that is too wide and resew at the proper ¼″. To correct fat snake channels you don't have to remove the stitches; just resew the seam a little wider, at an accurate and consistent ¼″.

■ Slope

If slope is not corrected before you tube the strata, you will create *torque*, a twist in the strata tube. This makes the tube unusable. Both strata ends must be cut at a 90° angle to the internal seams. (Figure 7-10A)

TO CHECK FOR SLOPE IN STRATA: Select a short line from the middle area of your ruler and place it on one of the internal seams near the center of the strata unit. The long edge of the ruler will be at a 90° angle to the end of the strata unit. If the end of the strata unit is traveling gradually away from 90° (the long edge of the ruler), it has slope. This can happen at either edge—top or bottom. Trim off any excess per Figure 7-10B.

TO CHECK FOR SLOPE IN BARGELLO WORK: Position ruler and trim as shown in Figure 7-10C.

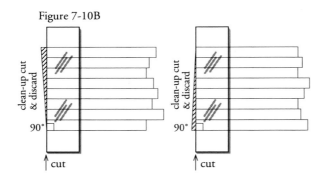

Figure 7-10B

clean-up cut & discard

90°

↑ cut

clean-up cut & discard

90°

↑ cut

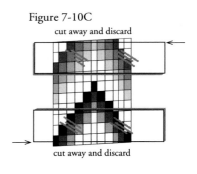

Figure 7-10C

cut away and discard

cut away and discard

■ Rainbows, lettuce leaves, and roller coasters

1. If the fabric at the edge of the strata unit rises away from or bellows off the edge of the table you have a "rainbow" arch (Figure 7-11).

2. If there are fluffy waves of excess fullness along one or both of the long outside edges of the strata unit you have "lettuce leaf" strata, also called "roller coaster edges"—the unit curves or ripples along the edges (Figure 7-12A & 7-12B).

Figure 7-11 "Rainbow Arch"

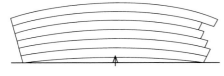

Figure 7-12A
Full at one edge–"Lettuce Leaf"

Figure 7-12B
"Lettuce Leaves" at both edges

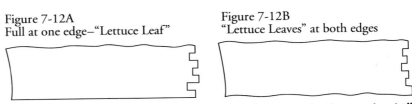

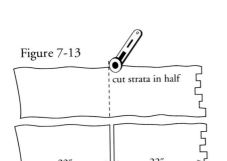

Figure 7-13

cut strata in half

22"   22"

If your strata unit has rainbows, lettuce leaves, or both, cut the 45" unit in half top to bottom to make two 22" units (Figure 7-13). With right sides together fold the two units in half on an internal seam. Make a 90° clean-up cut at both ends of each unit, a total of four cuts (Figure 7-14). NOTE: *If twisting develops after you have tubed a strata unit, open the tube seam, refold on a seam near the center, make another clean-up cut at 90° and retube the remaining strata. Don't fret — you have only cut away distortion, not the good, useful areas.*

Figure 7-14

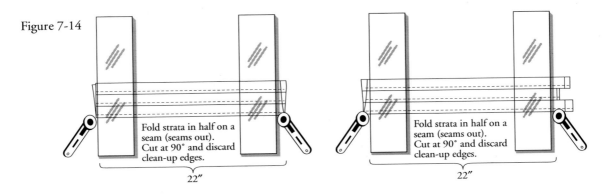

Fold strata in half on a seam (seams out).
Cut at 90° and discard clean-up edges.

22"

Fold strata in half on a seam (seams out).
Cut at 90° and discard clean-up edges.

22"

3. It would be good to review this chapter on how to:
    A. Cut straight strips,
    B. Sew without distortion,
    C. Iron accurately,
    D. Discover the need for a machine tune-up or adjustment, and
    E. Eliminate thread-weight distortions.

so these "Check and Correct" efforts are less frequent and less challenging for you in the future.

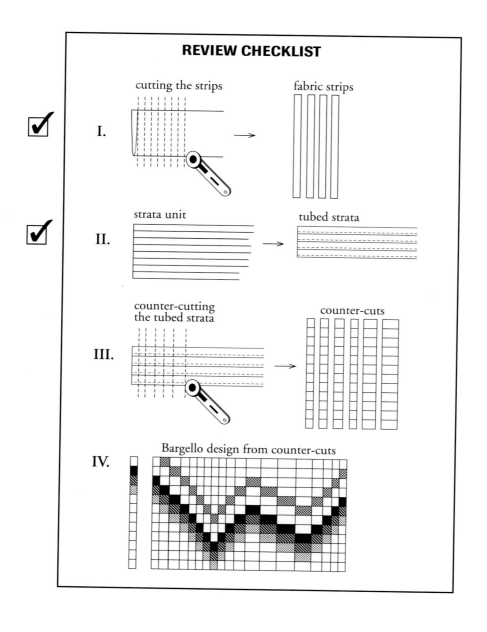

REVIEW CHECKLIST

I. cutting the strips → fabric strips

II. strata unit → tubed strata

III. counter-cutting the tubed strata → counter-cuts

IV. Bargello design from counter-cuts

C O L O R   G A L L E R Y

See **Appendix B** for yardage and cutting information.

1. ***Southwest Canyon*** (from Grand Canyon Series) by Louise Harris
    62″ x 44″ (Sequential)

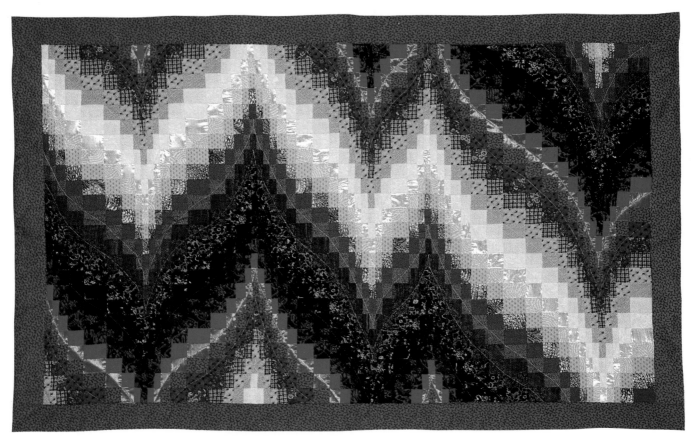

2. *Turquoise Tapestry* by Diane Becka, 28″ x 48″ (Sequential)

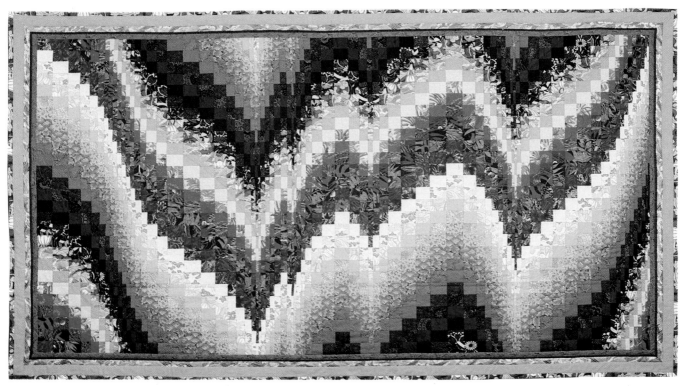

3. *Magic Mountains* by Louise Harris, 84" x 49" (Sequential)

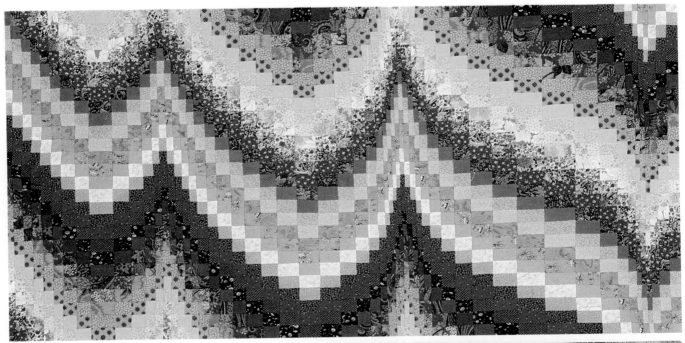

4. ***Double Valance S Curve*** by Marilyn
   Doheny 26″ x 56″ (Sequential)

4b. (right) Fabric detail

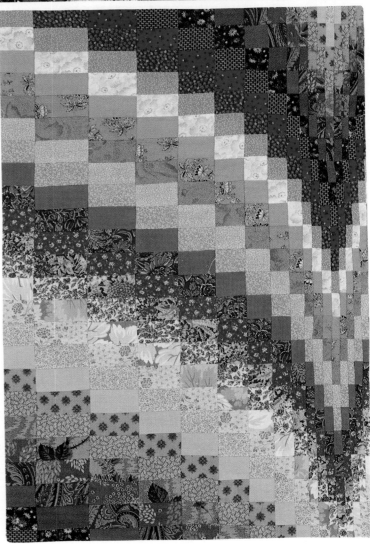

5. *Majesty* by Donna Van Buren, 46" x 55" (Sequential)

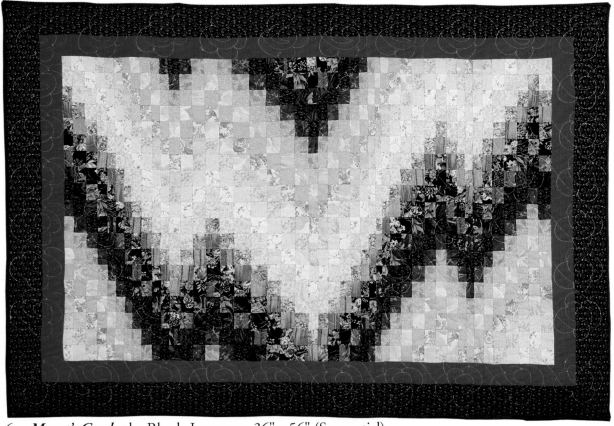

6. *Monet's Garden* by Rhoda Lonergan, 36" x 56" (Sequential)

7. *Flower Garden* by Alice Rudolph, 18" x 25", (Sequential)

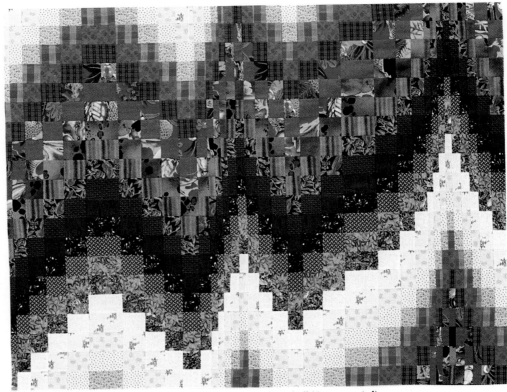

8. *Asphalt Jungle* by Vivian Larson, 60H" x 49" (Sequential)

9. *Sparkling Water* by Sally Lindman, 21" x 30" (Sequential)
    (top edge of quilt is indicated by asterisk)

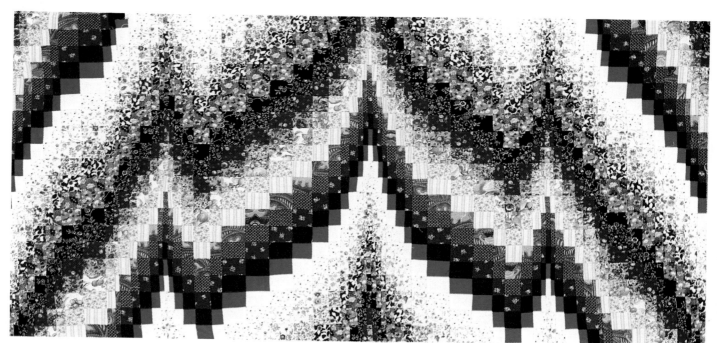

10. *Garden Arches* by Marilyn Doheny, 20″ x 40″ (Symmetrical sequential)

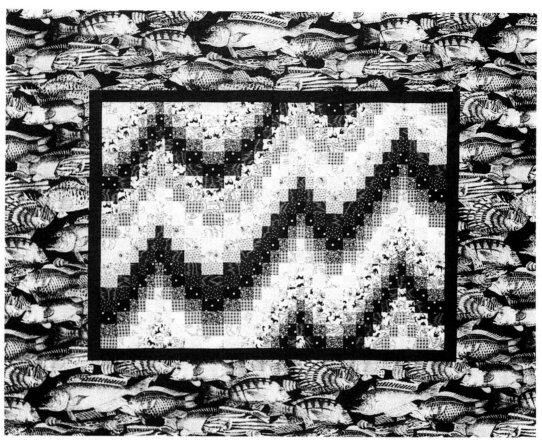

11. *Fish Ladder* by Janet Kime, 45" x 60" (Sequential)

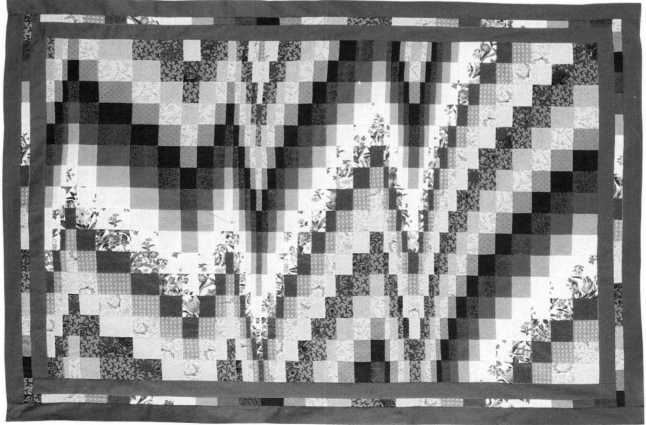

12. *First Ascent* by Robin Teal, 38" x 56" (Sequential)

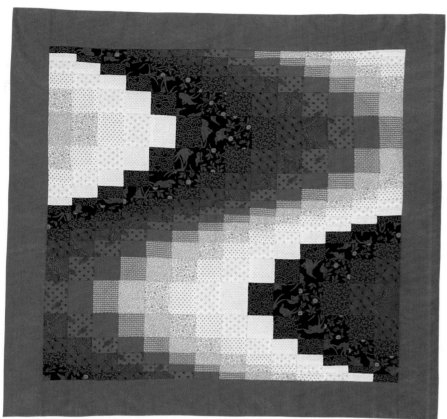

13. *Yin Yang* by Diane Becka,
25" x 25" (Sequential)

14. *Anniversary Blessings*
by Robin Strobel
King size (Sequential
with river spacer)
fabric detail only

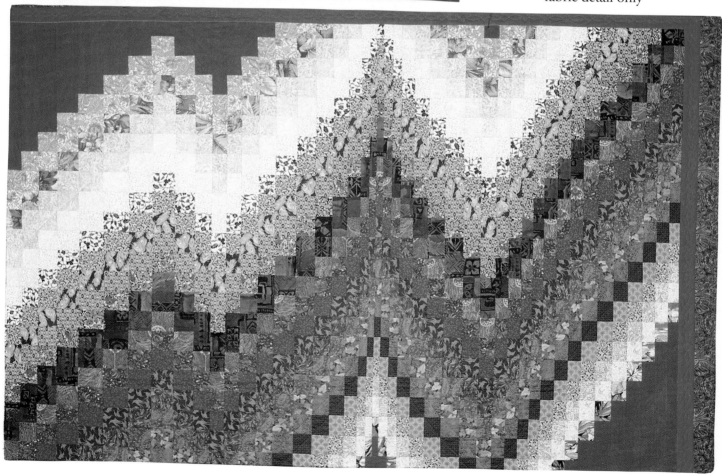

15. *Painted Desert* by Maribeth Donner, 37" x 65" (Double Repeat)

16. *My Pink Garden*
    by Marilyn Doheny
    33″ x 26″
    (Double Repeat)

*

17. *Matilda's Music* by Joan Blair, owned by MaryAnn Schmidt, 80" x 70"
    (Double Repeat)   (top edge of quilt is indicated by asterisk)

18. *Cherry Pie*
    by Helen Wichern
    33″ x 35″
    (Double Repeat)

19. *Candy Mountains*
    by Patsi Hanseth
    46″ x 30″ (Double Repeat)

20. *Sweetness & Light*
    by Betty Ores
    45″ x 55″ (Double Repeat)

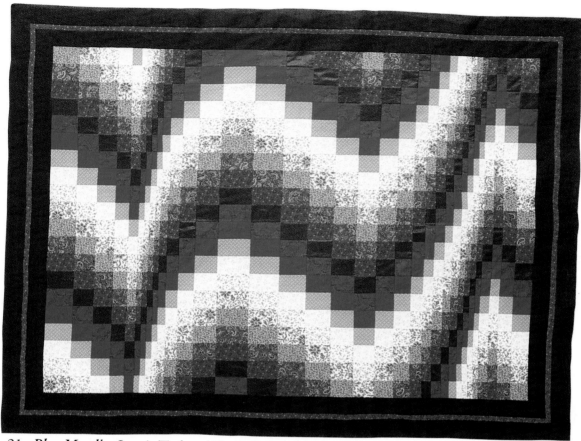

21. **Blue Mood** by Laurie Taylor, 46" x 56" (Double Repeat)

22. *Noël*
    by Marilyn Doheny
    30″ x 33″
    (Double Repeat)

23. ***That Old Yin Yang***
    by Janet Kime
    40" x 45"
    Printed striped fabric –
    tubed and shifted.
    (No strata made.)

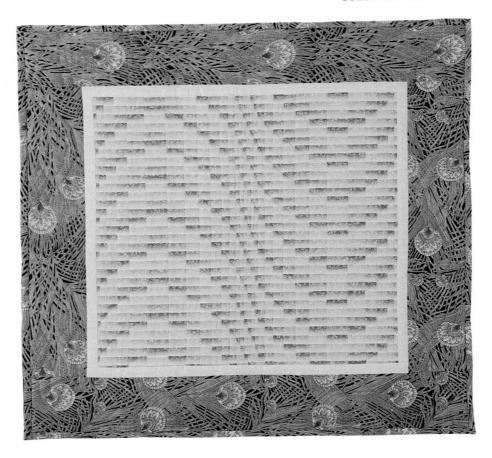

24. ***Madame Butterfly***
    by Marilyn Doheny
    44" x 44"
    (Prime Reverse Repeat)

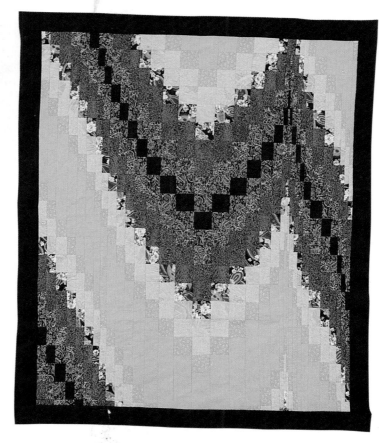

25. *From Issaquah with Love*
46" x 40"
(Contrived Reverse Repeat
with Island Spacer)

25b. Detail (above)

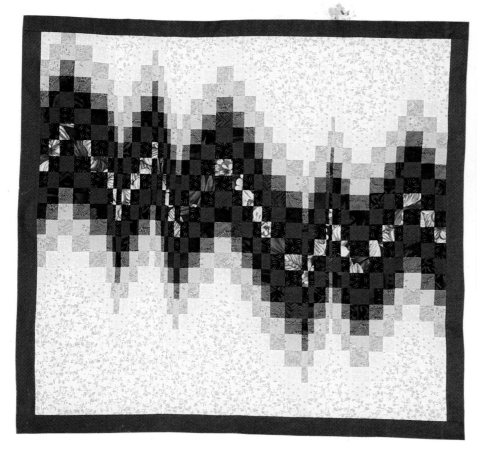

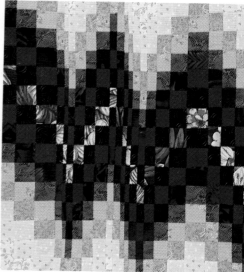

26. *My River In The Forest*
by Marjorie Lorant
45" x 50" (Contrived
Reverse Repeat with
Background Spacer)

26b. Detail (above)

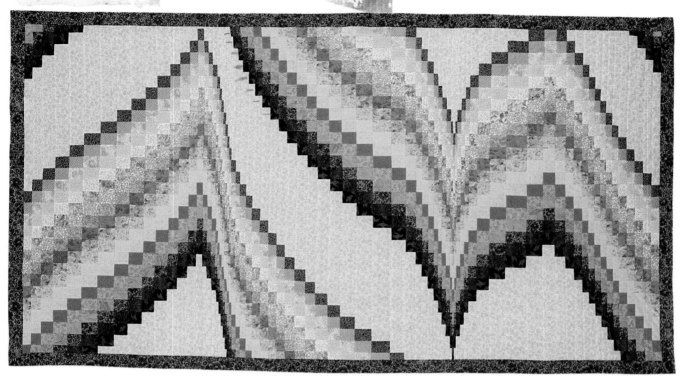

27. *Desert Palisades* by Shelley Nelson, 50" x 70" (Sequential with River Spacer)

28. *Blue Arches* by Mary Beth Donner, 40" x 55" (Repeated with River Spacer)

*

29. *Birds In Flight* by Susan Gordon, 35" x 50" (Sequential with River Spacer and half staggers)
   (top edge of quilt is indicated by asterisk)

30. *Delicate Sensations* by Stephanie Newman
   90″ x 70″ (Repeated with 2 River Spacers)

31. *Misty Morning Memories of Monet* by Vivian Heiner, 50" x 59"
    (Sequential with River Spacer)

32. *Mountain Waterfall*
    by Leone Newman
    90″ x 80″
    (Sequential with River Spacer)

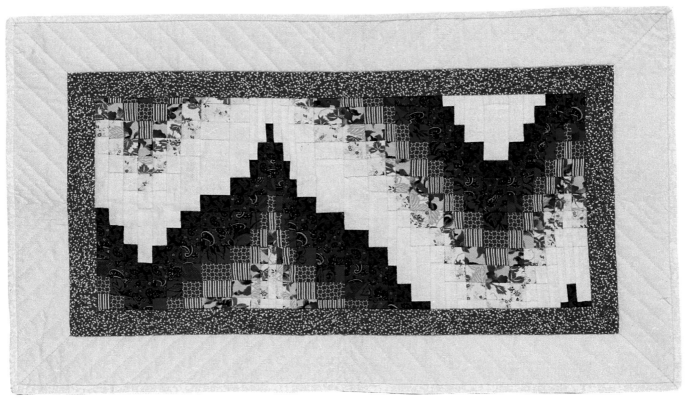

33. *Red River Valley* by Marilyn Doheny, 15" x 30" (Sequential with River Spacer)

34. *Vacation Memories*
by Nell Moynihan
38″ x 38″ (Sequential
with 2 River Spacers)

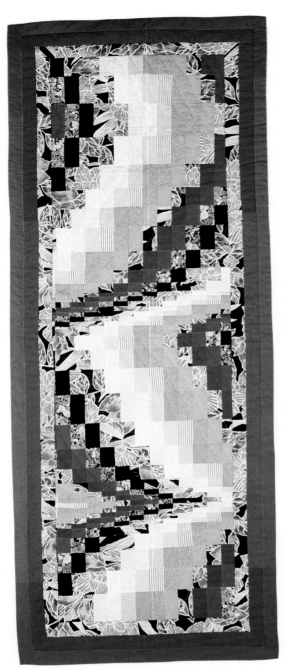

35. *Contemporary Images* by Evie Newell
22″ x 52″ (Sequential with River Spacer)

36. *Presidential Suite* by Eloise Benedict
15″ x 30″ (Sequential with River Spacer)

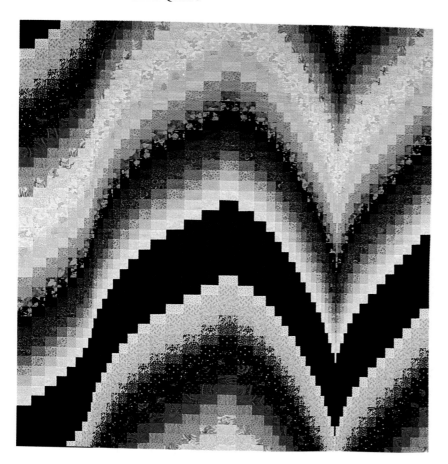

37. *Heat Wave*
    by Nancy Mahoney
    60″ x 55″
    (Sequential with
    2 River Spacers)

38. *Crazy Days of Summer* or
    Upstream Salmon
    by Nell Clinton–Moynihan
    40″ x 36″ (Sequential with River
    Spacer)

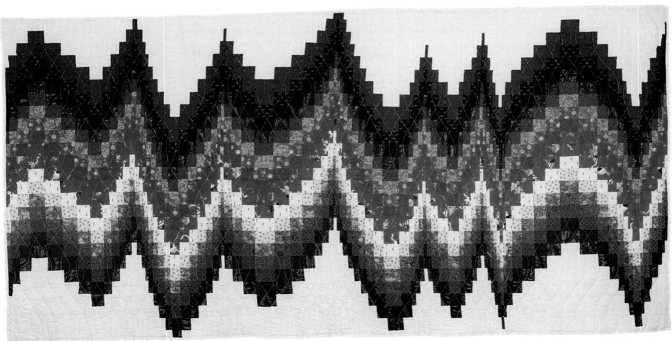

39. *Christmas Banner* by Marilyn Doheny and Sue Pilarski, 50″ x 100″ (Sequential with Background Spacer)

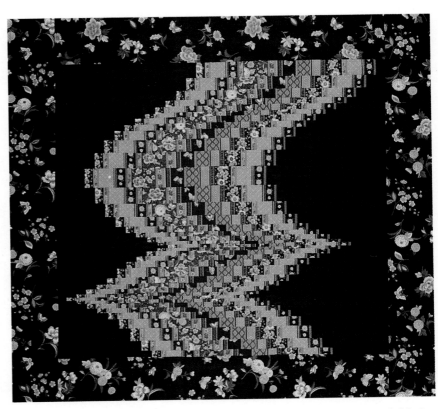

40. *Untitled* by Janet Kime, 50" x 50" (One printed striped fabric with Background Spacer)

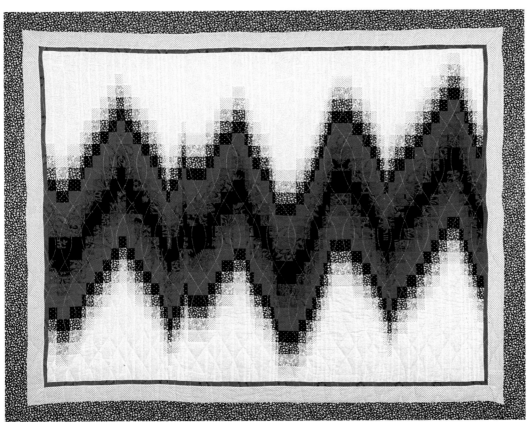

41. *Heart Monitor* by Mary E. Fox, 55" x 65" (Reverse Repeat with Background Spacer)

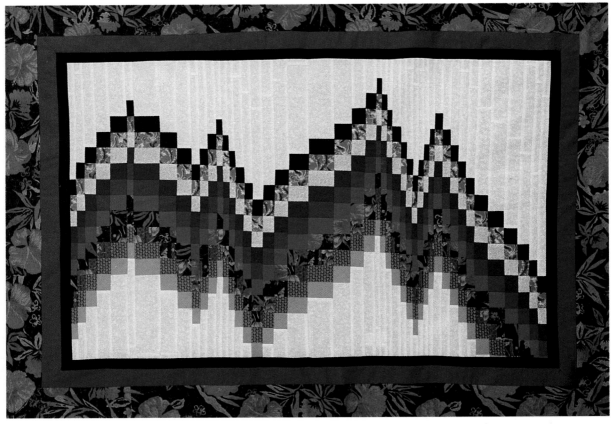

42. *Reflections of Lahaina* by Diane Strand, 38" x 55" (Sequential with Background Spacer)

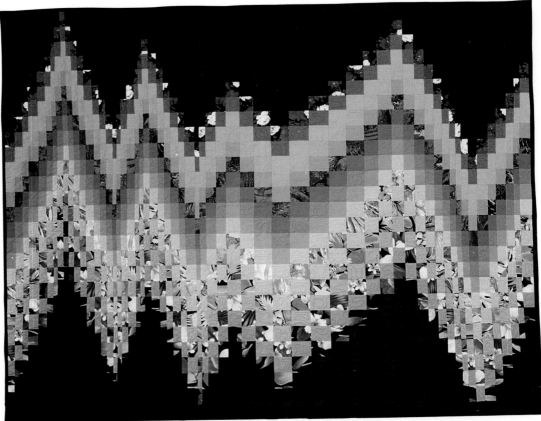

43. *Larry's Dream* by Joel Patz, 55" x 75" (Sequential with Background Spacer)

44. *My Purple Valances*
by Marilyn Doheny
27" x 30"
(Repeat with
Background Spacer)

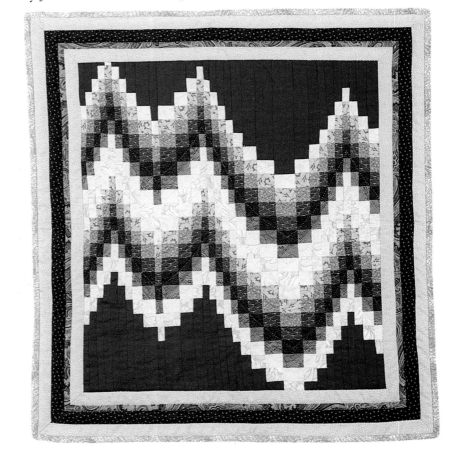

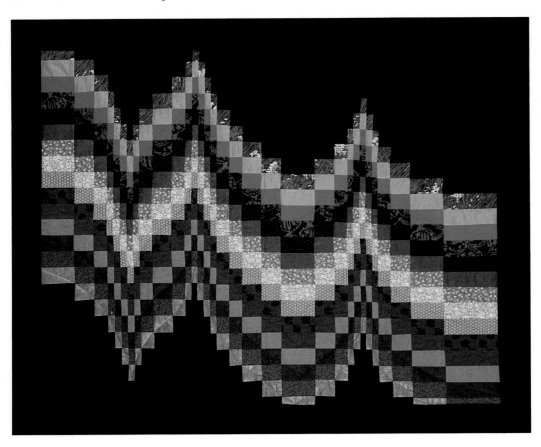

45. ***Ooh La La***
by Diane Becka
52″ x 64″
(Sequential with
Background
Spacer)

46. ***Harbor Grays*** by Vivian Heiner, 44" x 58" (Sequential with Island Spacer)

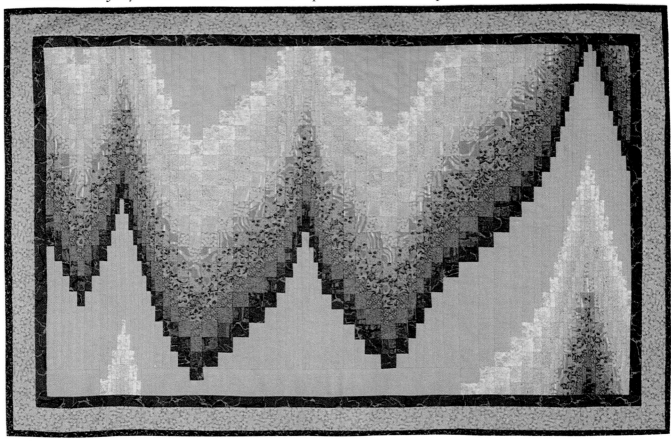

47. ***A River Runs Through It***
by Sheila Hopkins
38″ x 30″
(Sequential with Island Spacer)

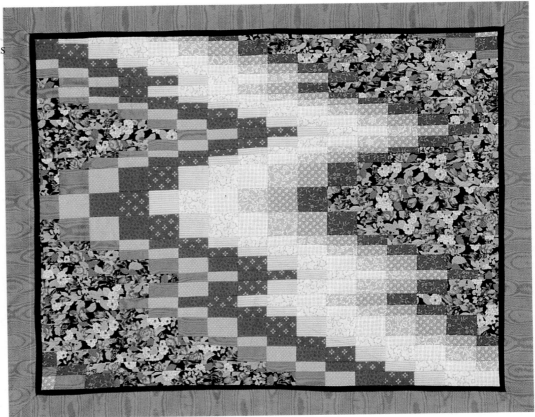

48. ***Mountain Meadows, B.C.*** by Emilie Belak, 66" x 96"
(Sequential with one River Spacer and one Island Spacer)

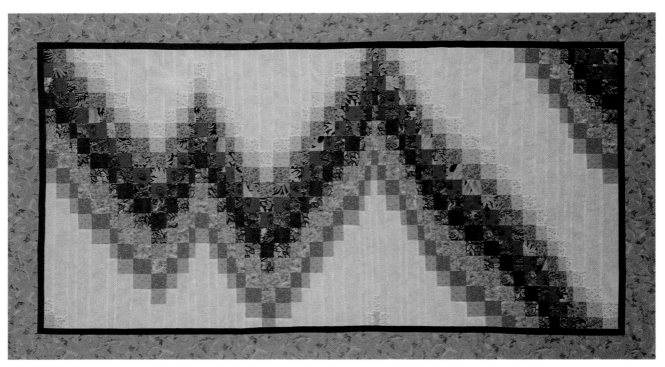

49. *Spinning My Dreams* by Ola Booknight, 40" x 60" (Sequential with Island Spacer)

50. *Above The Fruited Plains*
by Rhoda Lonergan
45″ x 55″ (Sequential with
Island Spacer)

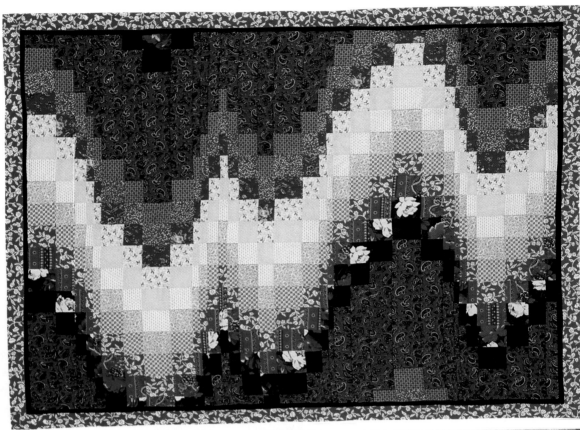

51. *(above)*
Joan Loves Red
by Dawn Coons,
30″ x 45″ (Sequential
with Island Spacer)

52. *(right)*
May God Grant Prayers
by Lynn Boland
72″ x 72″ (Sequential
with Island Spacer)

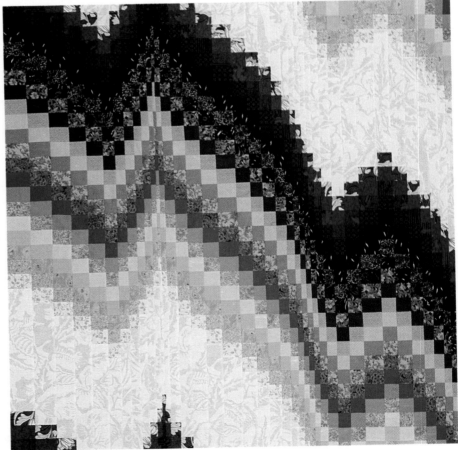

53. *Kabouki Island* by Marilyn Doheny
    48″ x 48″ (Reverse Repeat
    with Island Spacer)

54. *My Floral Jungle* by Arlene Schekler
    45″ x 30″
    (Reverse Repeat with River Spacer)

55. *#1 Son* by Rhoda Lonergan
   80″ x 70″ (Sequential with 1 River Spacer and Vertical Interruptions)

56. *Graded Bars*
by Diane Becka
51″ x 55″
(Sequential with
Vertical
Interruptions)

57. *Fire & Ice On My Bed*
by Maribeth Donner
120″ x 120″
(Sequential with
Vertical Interruptions)

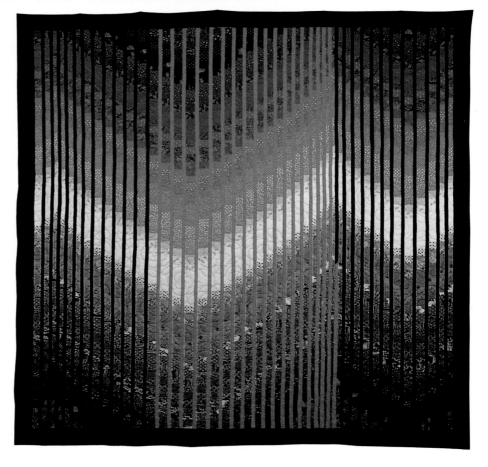

58. *(above)*
Rory's Jungle Quilt
by Muriel Neale
50″ x 76″
(Sequential with
Vertical Interruptions)

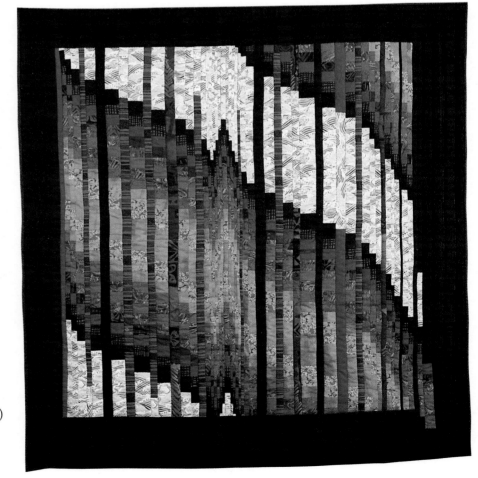

59. *(right)*
Jonathan L.S.
by Vivian Heiner
60″ x 66″
(Reverse Repeat with
2 River Spacers and
Vertical Interruptions)

60. *Amazing Grace* by Vivian Heiner, 25″ x 40″
(Sequential with 2 Spacers and Vertical Pleats)

TUBING THE STRATA AND COUNTER-CUTTING

Regardless of the strata style you have at this point—whether it is repeat, reverse-repeated, or sequential, and whether it includes a spacer section or not — you will create a tube from the strata unit and counter-cut it at various widths to create the Bargello design.

Thin counter-cuts cause the design to move quickly and vertically in the up and down directions, while wider counter-cuts cause the design to move slower with more sweeping side-to-side horizontal direction. These changes in the speed and direction of the movement add contrast that is sensuous and dramatic. Whatever motion you prefer, you can create it any time you wish to do so. A dynamic and effective quilt design has many pulsations, movements, and sensations contained within its flow.

TUBING THE STRATA UNITS

> **REMINDER:** Before the strata units are tubed, iron equal amounts of strata in opposite directions. It is much easier to check for this now than after the strata have been sewn into tubes.

First clean up both ends of each strata unit so they are at right angles to the center seam. To do this easily:

a) Fold the strata unit in half lengthwise, right sides together, on the seamline nearest the center of the unit (Figures 8-1B & 8-2B).

b) Position your ruler and make a 90° clean-up cut as close to each end of the strata unit as possible. Every fabric in the unit should be included in

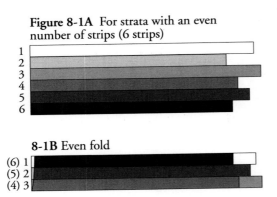

Figure 8-1A For strata with an even number of strips (6 strips)

8-1B Even fold

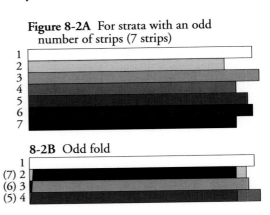

Figure 8-2A For strata with an odd number of strips (7 strips)

8-2B Odd fold

Figure 8-3

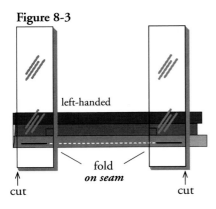

left-handed

fold
on seam

cut   cut

the trim to create 90° and to remove all of the selvedges (Figure 8-3).

c) If the long edges of the first and last fabrics remain parallel the entire length of the strata unit when folded, you can sew their long edges together to create a tube (Figure 8-5).

d) If they are not parallel, there is a distortion; the strata must be cut in half at about 22" center (Figure 8-4A). The two ends and the two middle areas will then be cleaned up to 90° from a center seam (Figure 8-4B). Follow the instructions under "Rainbows, lettuce leaves, and roller coasters" in Chapter 7 for details.

Figure 8-4A

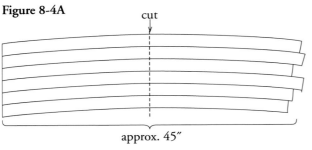

cut

approx. 45"

Figure 8-4B

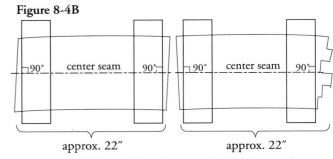

90°   center seam   90°   90°   center seam   90°

approx. 22"   approx. 22"

Figure 8-5

sew →

To tube the strata unit, fold it right sides together and sew the long edge of the first fabric to the long edge of the last fabric (Figure 8-5).

If the tube is large enough to allow the end of your ironing board inside it, as if it were a sleeve, press the seam allowance in the same direction as the others in the strata unit. If not, allow this one seam to remain unironed.

NOTE: Once the strata units have been tubed, it is difficult to tell the ones which were ironed up from the ones which were ironed down. Learn to identify them from the direction a particular pair of fabrics is ironed—for example, from **blue** to **pink** in one strata and from **pink** to **blue** in the other. Or from **fish** to **flowers** and from **flowers** to **fish.**

MAKING COUNTER-CUTS IN THE TUBES

Counter-cuts will always be made alternately from two different strata tubes—each with its seams ironed the opposite of the other strata. The only exception is when vertical interruptions are going to be used. Then all seams can conveniently go down.

1. With the seam allowances on the outside of each tube, make the 90° counter-cuts in the strata units one at a time, alternating between them.
2. Use one of the internal seamlines and check the 90° angle frequently. Trim to 90° whenever necessary.
3. The width of each counter-cut is determined by your design choice.

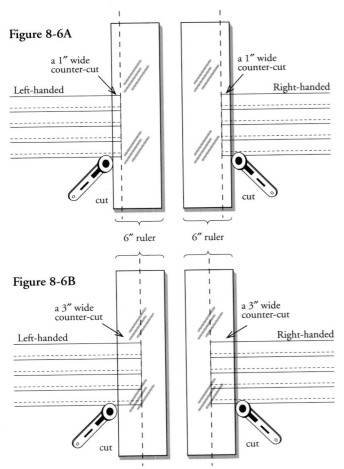

Figure 8-6A

a 1″ wide counter-cut

Left-handed

Right-handed

a 1″ wide counter-cut

cut   cut

6″ ruler   6″ ruler

Figure 8-6B

a 3″ wide counter-cut

Left-handed

Right-handed

a 3″ wide counter-cut

cut   cut

Position the long lines of the ruler position at the end of the strata unit; use them to measure the widths of the counter-cuts. Figures 8-6A & B show a 1″ wide and 3″ wide cuts respectively. Both left and right handed layouts are shown.

Each counter-cut will be opened by removing one of the seams between two fabrics. Handle the counter-cuts carefully, keeping the stitching as intact as possible, until the seam to be removed is determined.

If you have a Background spacer, no seams will be opened. Instead, the tube will be opened by cutting the spacer at different locations, counter-cut by counter-cut.

For River and Island spacers, a combination of seam opening and spacer cutting is used. For seam removal techniques see Chapter 9 for all strata types.

CREATING SQUARES AND RECTANGLES IN THE COUNTER-CUTS

■ Squares

Squares come from counter-cuts that have the same cut width as the original strips. For example, if the strata strips were cut 2″ wide, then 2″ counter-cuts will produce squares. The finished squares will be 1½″x 1½″ after all seams are taken (i.e., after the counter-cuts are sewn back together in the Bargello pattern).

■ Thin rectangles

Thin rectangles produce quick, vertical Bargello motion. The thinner the cuts and the longer the series of thin cuts, the more dramatic the effect. Thin counter-cuts produce steep, piercing, intense areas in a Bargello Tapestry quilt.

Figure 8-7
Sharp peaks from thin counter-cuts

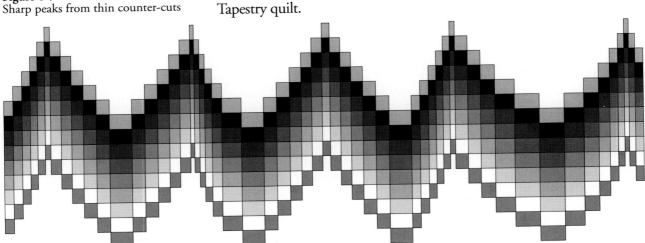

Thin rectangles come from counter-cuts that are more narrow than the cut width of the original strips. For example, if the strata strips were cut 2″ wide, then any counter-cut less than 2″ wide will produce thin rectangles. Figure 8-7 shows the effect of a series of counter-cuts that narrow by regular increments.

NOTE: The smallest possible cut width for a counter-cut is ¾″, which will produce rectangles that are only ¼″ wide after all seams are taken. If you made a counter-cut only ½″ wide, after you took a ¼″ seam allowance on each side there would be no exposed fabric. Ponder this for a while: *What would happen if you cut five ½″ strips and then sewed them together using ¼″ seams?* This amusing puzzle is fun to ponder!

■ Wide rectangles

Wide rectangles produce dramatic horizontal Bargello motion. The wider the cuts and the longer the series of wide cuts, the more dramatic the effect. Wide rectangles produce soft, billowy areas in a Bargello Tapestry quilt.

Wide rectangles come from counter-cuts that are wider than the cut width of the original strips. For example, if the strata strips were cut 2″ wide, then any counter-cut wider than 2″ will produce wide rectangles. Figure 8-8 shows a series of counter-cuts that widen by regular increments.

NOTE: I recommend that the widest counter-cut be up to but no more than 2½ times the original cut width of the strips. For example, if the cut width of the strips is 2″, I would recommend a maximum counter-cut width of 2″ x 2½″ = 5″, which would be 4½″ wide after seam allowances are taken.

Figure 8-8
Billowy

■ Rule-of-Thumb Chart for Maximum Width Counter-Cuts

Original Strata Strips cut size	Widest Counter-Cut cut size
1½″	3¾″
1¾″	4¾″
2″	5″
2¼″	5¾″
2½″	6¼″
2¾″	6¾″
3″	7½″
3¼″	8¼″
3½″	8¾″
3¾″	9¼″
4″	10″
4¼″	10½″

After 4¼″ strips, I drop the rule-of-thumb ratio and use proportions that I find acceptable. They are each less than 2½ times the original cut width. Use whichever you like. *Don't avoid wide countercuts—they create contrasting drama and make the thin ones seem thinner!*

4½″	10½″
4¾″	11″
5″	11″
5¼″	11″
5½″	11″
5¾″	11½″
6″	12″

It is the proportion between the width of the fabric strips and the width of the counter-cuts that determines the movement of the Bargello design. Figures 8-9A and 8-9B show two quilts with identical movement, even though the strips and counter-cuts are different sizes.

Figure 8-9A

Arrows point to counter-cuts of 2″ x 2″ squares

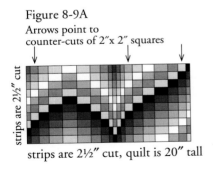

strips are 2½″ cut, quilt is 20″ tall

Figure 8-9B

Arrows point to counter-cuts of 4″ x 4″ squares

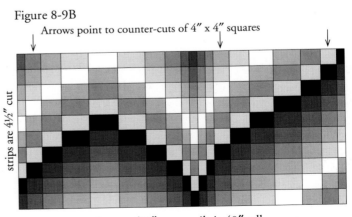

strips are 4½″ cut, quilt is 40″ tall

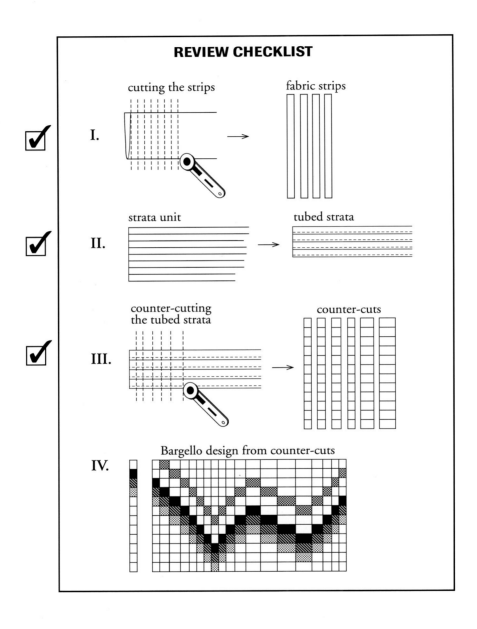

REVIEW CHECKLIST

I. cutting the strips → fabric strips

II. strata unit → tubed strata

III. counter-cutting the tubed strata → counter-cuts

IV. Bargello design from counter-cuts

C H A P T E R   9

STRATA INTO BARGELLO MOVEMENT

Regardless of the strata style you have at this point—whether it is repeated, reverse-repeated, or sequential, or whether it includes a spacer section or not—you will next create a tube with the strata and make counter-cuts of various widths. *Any counter-cut that is equal to the original strip width will create squares, thinner counter-cuts produce vertical rectangles, and wider counter-cuts produce horizontal rectangles.* Using all of the counter-cut widths is essential to the drama and sensuousness of the design. Most people are too cautious and fail to include a full range of widths, from very thin to very wide. Be more dramatic using thinner and thicker counter-cut widths than feels comfortable to you and your Bargello Tapestry quilt will be more spectacular for the risk. Be dramatic!

The up and down motion itself is created differently depending on whether the strata has a spacer section or not. With no spacer to contend with, the tubes are usually opened by removing a seam between two fabrics. If a spacer is involved, the spacer needs to be cut into when it hits the top or the bottom edge of the Bargello movement, releasing some spacer to be at each edge, top and bottom.

Any individual counter-cut is not going to make or break the quilt. Creating overall motion, counter-cut by counter-cut, is the process of building a total design. An upward motion *sweep* requires three or more counter-cuts, side-by-side, going in an upward direction. A downward motion *sweep* is created by three or more counter cuts, side-by-side, going in a downward direction. The width of the counter-cuts should appeal to your sense of quickness or loftiness or billowiness, and certainly adding more than three in a sweep is the desired choice.

You can also choose to drop a full strip width, drop less and that for a partial stagger, or more than a full width for an extended stagger (slub). Each spacer style also produces a different effect as the spacer moves within the emerging design. Understanding each of these categories; 1) **up and down movement,** 2) **with or without a spacer,** 3) **the degree of the stagger** and 4) **thick square or thin** — will help you define your choices.

Figure 9-1

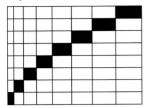

Figure 9-2

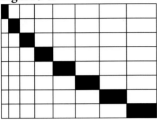

Figure 9-4 Full Drop
For full stagger downward to the right the next 3 openings would be as indicated.

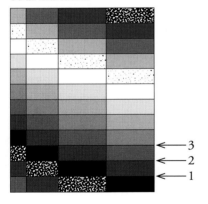

← 3
← 2
← 1

Figure 9-5A Partial Drop
For half stagger downward to the right, the next 3 openings would be as indicated.

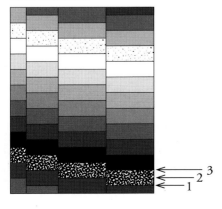

← 2 3
← 1

The delight is that you have infinite options. Learning to use them is simply becoming a master gardener in your own exquisite garden.

UP AND DOWN MOTION—IN A NUTSHELL

Movement in a Bargello Tapestry design comes from counter-cuts placed side by side so that the position of any individual fabric in the strata moves either up or down. Reading from left to right, upward motion is created by three or more counter-cuts moving in an upward direction (Figure 9-1). Downward motion is created by three or more counter-cuts moving in a downward direction (Figure 9-2). When three or more counter-cuts move in one direction the movement is called a *sweep*. For example, Figure 9-3 has seven sweeps. A successful Bargello design usually includes several sweeps. You must have at least 3 sweeps in your design before you can expect to see Bargello movement; you will probably want to include a much larger number of sweeps.

Figure 9-3

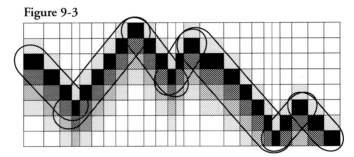

UP AND DOWN MOTION WITHOUT SPACERS

Full and Partial Drops

As described in the last chapter, the speed of motion (high/low as well as left to right) in a Bargello design is determined by the width of the counter-cuts. It is also affected by the amount of *drop* each counter-cut creates. Drop is the distance each fabric moves relative to the last counter-cut.

A *full drop* is created when each successive counter-cut: A) opens on a seam and B) moves up or down one full strip size. The corners of each individual fabric touch row by row in the design, the design is relatively pronounced, and motion is relatively rapid. All up and down motion is the full height of each fabric strip. Each tube opens on a seam. For full drops (Figure 9-4), the next three counter-cuts to the right, going downward, would open on seam #1 first, seam #2 second, and seam #3 third.

A *partial drop* is created when counter-cuts move up and down *less than* the height of one fabric strip. Every other counter-cut opens on a seam but alternate (in-between) counter-cuts open by cutting into a fabric. While full drops look like stairsteps, partial drops are less sharply defined and the edges of each fabric piece seem slightly blurred. The design tends to be flatter and the up and down motion is more gradual. For partial drops (Figure 9-5), the next

Figure 9-5B Slub
The next 3 openings
could be as indicated.

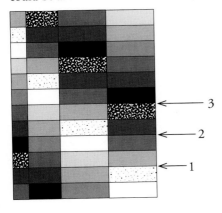

three counter-cuts to the right going downward would open on seam #1 for the first, cut into a fabric at point #2 for the second, and open on seam #3 for the third.

A **slub** is created when counter-cuts move up and down *more than* a full drop. The tube can be opened on seams or cut into, anywhere desired.

Areas of color or value act as a unit and can be aggressively moved high and low while still apearing to interact. This is the quickest technique to produce high and low movenement. To do this you make visual choices as desired, line up your feature fabrics in the tube with the same fabrics at the edge of the design, move as desired until pleased. Then roll the remaining area of the tube to the edge and open the tube at this place either on seam or by cutting a fabric apart. Example 9-5B shows regular drops but by more than one seam each time.

NOTE: It is possible to mix and match all three styles in one quilt!

Figure 9-6 Upward Motion

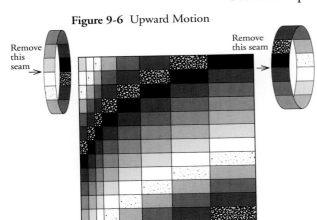

Remove
this
seam

Remove
this seam

Opening the Tube

The strata unit is tubed to make it easier to design with each counter-cut. If the strata unit were not tubed, it would be necessary to remove fabrics from one end of each counter-cut and sew them to the other end. Instead, with a tubed strata unit you simply remove one seam to open it up, perfectly integrated. With each new counter-cut, determine which seam to remove, within the tube, by following specific information for upward and downward motion.

■ Upward Motion

To determine where to open a tube for upward motion, look at the previous counter-cut. Find the two fabrics *at the top*. Find these same two fabrics in the tube and remove the seam *between* them (Figure 9-6). **Do this carefully so you don't pop open other seams.** The fabric which was at the top of the last row will be at the bottom of the new row (Figure 9-7). All of the other fabrics will automatically move up one position when the counter-cuts are merged (Figure 9-8).

Figure 9-7

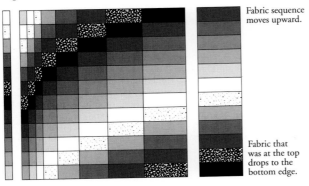

Fabric sequence
moves upward.

Fabric that
was at the top
drops to the
bottom edge.

Figure 9-8 Merged

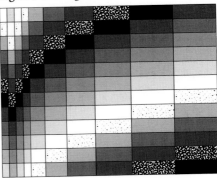

Figure 9-9 For Downward Motion

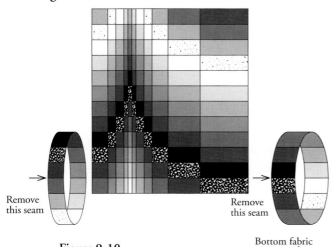

Remove
this seam

Remove
this seam

■ Downward Motion

To determine where to open a tube for downward motion, look at the previous counter-cut. Find the two fabrics *at the bottom.* Find these same two fabrics in the tube and remove the seam *between* them (Figure 9-9). ***Do this carefully so you don't pop open other seams.*** The fabric which was at the bottom of the last row will be at the top of the new row (Figure 9-10). All of the other fabrics will automatically move down one position when the counter-cuts are merged (Figure 9-11).

Figure 9-10

Bottom fabric
moves to the
top edge.

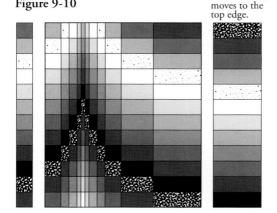

Fabric sequence
moves downward

Figure 9-11   Merged

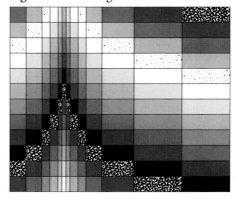

■ Partial Drops

A partial drop is created when the next counter-cut is moved up or down *less than one strip height.* The seams do not intersect. The design tends to be flatter and more mushy (Figure 9-12). The up and down motion is more gradual. *A partial drop is created* **on seam** *every other tube opening and* **mid-fabric** *on alternate tube openings by cutting the fabric with scissors rather than opening a seam* (Figures 9-13 & 9-14).

Figure 9-12
Partial Drop (1/2 stagger)

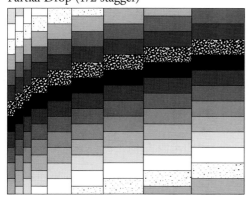

Figure 9-13 Up

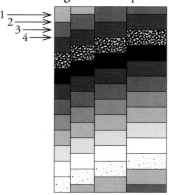

2 + 4 *open* a seam

Figure 9-14 Down

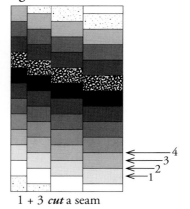

1 + 3 *cut* a seam

UP AND DOWN MOTION WITH SPACERS

■ Background spacer

When there is a *background spacer* in your strata unit, it will always appear above and below your Bargello design. Each tube is opened by cutting the spacer fabric. At the most extreme ends of the up and down motion, the seam which joins the spacer to the strata strips can be opened. *If a cut is ever needed within 1″ of a spacer seam,* **open the seam instead of cutting the spacer.** Do not remove any of the seams between strata strips, or you will produce *islands* (see Option below).

■ To determine where to cut open a counter-cut

Look at the most recent row of the design (the last counter-cut). Find the three fabrics at the top of the design, just under the spacer. Place the counter-cut, still tubed, next to the last row and align the top three fabrics of the design with the same three fabrics in the counter-cut (Figure 9-15). Now follow the Upward and Downward information for specific details.

Figure 9-15

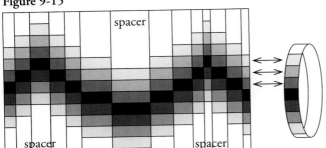

UPWARD MOTION: To create upward motion:

1) Align 3 fabrics (Figure 9-16).
2) Reposition the tube—move it upward so that all three of the fabrics are relocated one position upward (Figure 9-17).
3) Holding these fabrics in place, push or roll the excess portion of the tube upward until edge of the tube reaches the edge of the existing Bargello design.
4) Cut the spacer parallel to the counter-cut seams, approximately even with the top of the quilt. Scissors are easier than a rotary cutter for this cut.
5) Sew the counter-cut in place (Figure 9-18).
6) The next row of *upward* movement would open on the seam.

Figure 9-16
Aligned

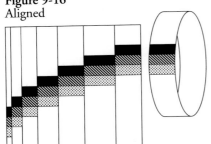

Figure 9-17
Moved 1 position up

Figure 9-18
New counter-cut in place

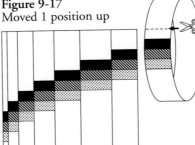

DOWNWARD MOTION: To create downward motion:

1) Align fabrics (Figure 9-19).
2) Reposition the tube—move it downward so that all three of the fabrics are relocated one position downward (Figure 9-20).
3) Holding these fabrics in place, push or roll the excess portion of the tube until an edge of the tube reaches the edge of the existing Bargello design.
4) Cut the spacer parallel to the counter-cut seams, at that location. Scissors are easier than a rotary cutter for this cut.
5) Sew the counter-cut in place (Figure 9-21).

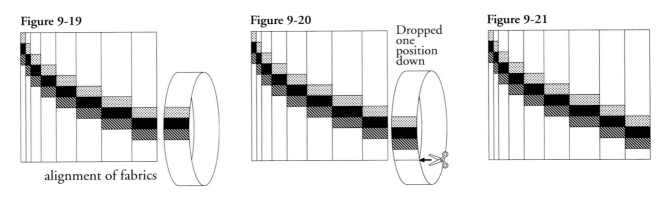

Figure 9-19

alignment of fabrics

Figure 9-20

Dropped one position down

Figure 9-21

NOTE: Because you are making these cuts casually, the top and bottom edges of the counter-cuts will be uneven. Do not match these edges as you sew the counter-cuts together; instead, match the internal seams and start the seam from the edge, however it aligns (Figure 9-22A). After you have sewn together all of the counter-cuts and pressed the quilt top, trim the top and bottom edges to 90° to create straight edges and an overall square or rectangular quilt top (Figure 9-22D).

ISLAND SPACERS: If you originally chose a Background Spacer and now wish to create Islands it is easy to change. The Bargello design will

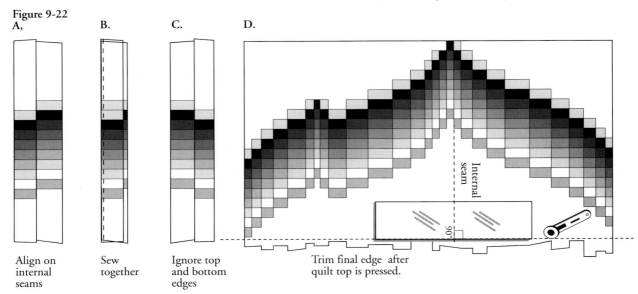

Figure 9-22

A,

B.

C.

D.

Align on internal seams

Sew together

Ignore top and bottom edges

Internal seam

90°

Trim final edge after quilt top is pressed.

"escape" the Background Spacer and instantly produce Islands (Figure 9-23), some of the counter-cuts will be opened at seamlines and some will be cut within the spacer fabric. Follow the instructions for upward or downward motion and cut into tubes with a spacer section.

Figure 9-23 Island Spacer

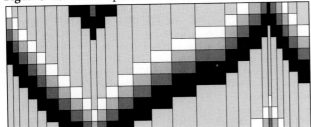

Figure 9-24 River Spacer

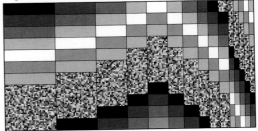

■ River and Island Spacers

River and Island spacers are not as wide as Background spacers, and do not entirely enclose the Bargello design (Figure 9-23 & 9-24). Depending on the movement created, each counter-cut is opened either by cutting the spacer fabric or by removing a seam between two fabric strips. Follow the previous instruction and illustrations for both styles.

NOTE: **If you need to make a "spacer fabric" cut within 1" of a seam, always open the seam instead of cutting the spacer.**

Again, the top and bottom edge will be uneven because you are making casual cuts. The edges are uneven for a second reason as well: opening a seam adds two ¼" seam allowances to the length of the counter-cut, while cutting the spacer fabric does not add any length to the counter-cut. Trim the edges after all counter-cuts have been sewn together and the quilt top has been pressed as in Figure 9-22D. Remember to interlock the seam to determine row by row sewing placement (Figure 9-22A) — not the top edges — because they are not necessarily even!

■ Moral support for trimming the top and bottom edges of the Bargello quilt

If you are worried about cutting off any portion of the quilt because you think the edge has the most beautiful and significant part of your quilt design, you are worrying needlessly. The body of what has been created is the most impressive area. Look back at each of the quilts photographed for this book. *Every one of them with a spacer at the edges was trimmed.* Can you see that anything is missing? Did you notice anything missing when you first looked through the book? Of course not!

To get into the proper mind set, pretend that you need to remove a bandage from a child's arm. For the least anxiety, you would remove the bandage quickly, making short work of it, and get on with activities that are more fun! The same mental approach is necessary here.

After the quilt top is finished and pressed, trim the top and bottom edges to match the shortest rows. Position the ruler at 90° to the quilt, using internal seams for alignment, and cut off the ¼"–½" excess along each top and bottom edge. Think quick and swift, then act with confidence and cut!

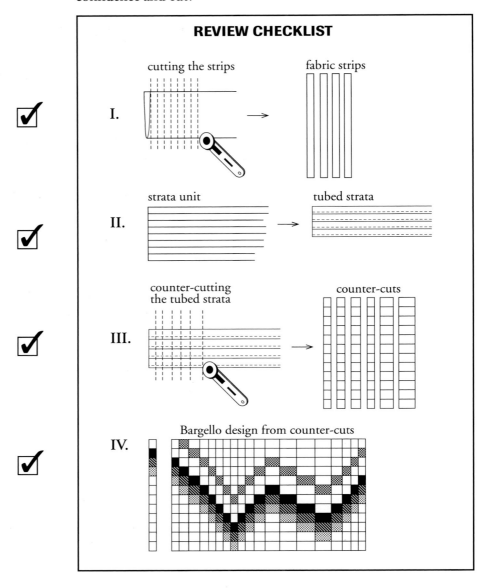

REVIEW CHECKLIST

I. cutting the strips → fabric strips

II. strata unit → tubed strata

III. counter-cutting the tubed strata → counter-cuts

IV. Bargello design from counter-cuts

C H A P T E R   10

BARGELLO PATTERN FLOW FOR ALL STYLES

As you develop the pattern of a Bargello Tapestry quilt, there are many choices you can make during the creative process—the design can be symmetrical or asymmetrical; worked upon itself or incorporate a spacer; it can have progressive flow or interrupted motion; have a full or partial drop; or it can be consecutively sewn or vertically interrupted in several ways. This chapter investigates all of these styles.

Page through the photographs of the quilts and study each one. Ask yourself which areas you like, as well as which areas you find unattractive. When you know what pleases and displeases you, it is easier to create that particular type of strata and flowing motion in your own quilt. Each quilt has been dissected so that its collective parts can be understood individually.

Regardless of which design elements you include, each Bargello Tapestry quilt develops simultaneously vertically and horizontally as each counter-cut is added. With each new counter-cut, there are three choices to make:

1. The width of the new counter-cut (thick or thin)
2. The motion of the new counter-cut (up or down)
3. The position of the new counter-cut (left or right)

SYMMETRICAL AND ASYMMETRICAL PATTERN FLOW

Symmetrical pattern flow means there is an obvious center to the Bargello design: the left half of the Bargello Tapestry quilt is the mirror image of

Figure 10-1
Symmetrical quilt with 10 sweeps

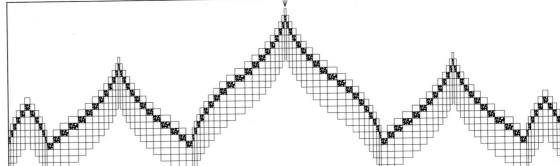

the right half. The quilt has a dead center, and counter-cut by counter-cut the widths and movements are identical on each side as they flow away from center (Figure 10-1).

Asymmetrical pattern flow means that the design has no dead center. The design continues to develop across the quilt. Each area of the design is independent of every other area (Figure 10-2).

Figure 10-2
Asymmetrical quilt
with seven sweeps

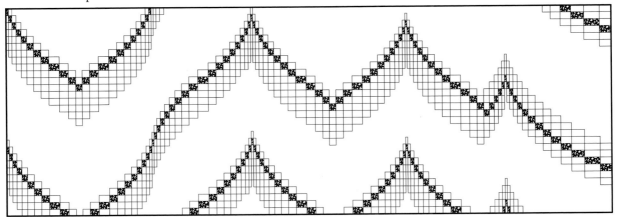

Figure 10-3
Follow the flow of the darkest fabric from left to right to see it walk off one edge and appear on the other.

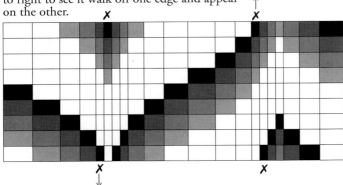

"WORKED UPON ITSELF" VS SPACERS

WORKED UPON ITSELF

A Bargello Tapestry quilt is *worked upon itself* if all the strips in the strata unit are the same width.

When a Bargello quilt is worked upon itself, all of the fabrics *scroll* through the entire design from the top to the bottom: as a fabric appears to "walk off" the bottom or top of the quilt, it immediately reappears on the opposite edge of the quilt, in the next row (Fig. 10-3).

SPACER

A *spacer* is an extra-wide strip of fabric sewn between two of the regular strips in the strata. The width of the spacer makes a dramatic difference in the effect the spacer has on the Bargello design.

■ River spacer

A River spacer gently influences the Bargello design, having the look of a thick river of fabric flowing within and around the Bargello pattern. It does not dramatically alter the effect or motion of the overall design. A River spacer is a fabric strip that is up to one-half the height (volume) of the strata unit. For example, if the strata unit is 30″ tall, a river spacer can be added and have up to 15″ size. The spacer is part of the tubed strata unit and can be placed anywhere among the strata strips (Figure 10-4).

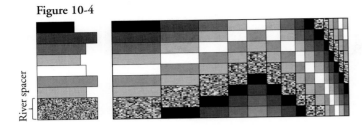

Figure 10-4

River spacer

■ Background spacer

A Background spacer is very large and very dramatic, and completely changes the Bargello design. A Background spacer fabric stays at the top and bottom of the Bargello design, completely surrounding the active movement. The Bargello design appears to float on the background fabric; hence the term, Background spacer. The cut width of a Background spacer is always equal to or larger than the total height of the strata unit. For example, if the strata unit is 30″ tall the background spacer can be added at 30″ or wider. The spacer should be placed at an outside edge of the strata strips (Fig. 10-5), as it actually stays in that area during pattern development, i.e., the top and bottom of the Bargello design, not flowing through it internally.

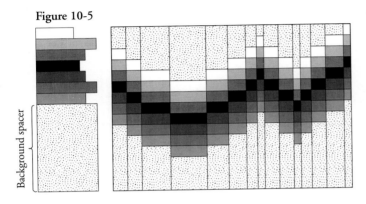

Figure 10-5

Background spacer

■ Island spacer

An Island spacer creates large islands of Bargello design. Island spacers are a combined effect somewhere between a River and a Background spacer: the appearance is as if a Background spacer decided not to contain the sweeping movement of the Bargello design and/or the river spacer grew and overflowed, creating floating islands of Bargello activity. An Island spacer varies between one-half and one whole strata height. For example, if the strata height is 30″ the island spacer that is added could be 16″ to 30″ wide (Figure 10-6).

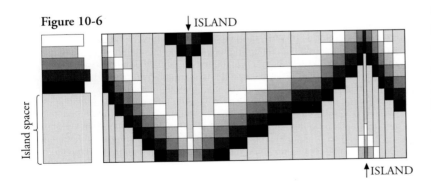

Figure 10-6   ↓ ISLAND

Island spacer

↑ ISLAND

PROGRESSIVE AND INTERRUPTED MOTION

A smoothly undulating Bargello Tapestry quilt has a series of "sweeps." A sweep is the movement between a high and low area. Sweeps can have *progressive* motion or *interrupted* motion. Progressive motion is a smooth flow within the sweeps. *Interrupted* motion, on the other hand, is a visually jarring ledge or checkerboard area of pattern flow within the sweep. Usually, at least three sweeps are necessary for Bargello movement to be impressive.

Figure 10-7
Progressive Motion

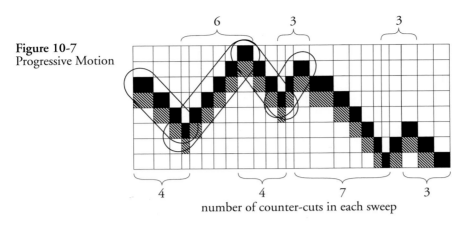

number of counter-cuts in each sweep

Figure 10-8A Progressive Motion
Gradually wider
1) 9 counter-cuts
2) all positioned to the right
3) all upward in motion

Figure 10-8B Progressive Motion
Gradually thinner
1) 9 counter-cuts
2) all positioned to the right
3) all upward in motion

PROGRESSIVE MOTION

Progressive motion is created in two different ways: a) by *gradually* changing the widths of the counter-cuts, and b) by using a *series* of more than three counter-cuts in each up or down sweep.

■ **How to Produce Progressive Motion (Figure 10-7)**
Width: Relative to the last counter-cut added, the next counter-cut should be either the same width, or an increase or decrease by any amount up to 1″. For example, an increase or decrease of ¼″, ½″, ¾″, 1″, or no change in width, would be progressive.

Motion: There must be at least three counter-cuts in every sweep. For example, an upward move requires at least three counter-cuts moving upward, one after the other, before adding a counter-cut to go downward. Figure 10-7 has seven sweeps, all of which have three or more counter-cuts in them. There is no maximum number of counter-cuts in one direction. The sweep is more elaborate and powerful when many counter-cuts work together (Figure 10-8, A-D).

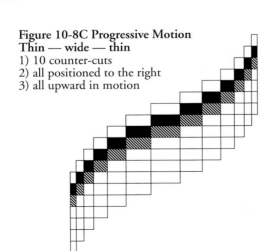

Figure 10-8C Progressive Motion
Thin — wide — thin
1) 10 counter-cuts
2) all positioned to the right
3) all upward in motion

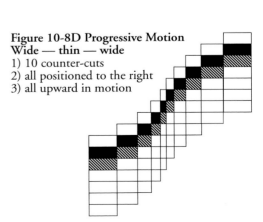

Figure 10-8D Progressive Motion
Wide — thin — wide
1) 10 counter-cuts
2) all positioned to the right
3) all upward in motion

Figure 10-9A
Interrupted Motion

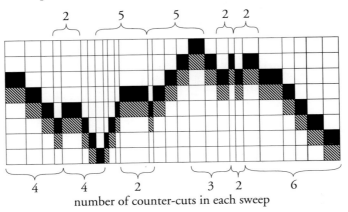

number of counter-cuts in each sweep

INTERRUPTED MOTION (Figure 10-9A)

Interrupted motion is the opposite of progressive motion, and is achieved by more adventurous changes in the counter-cut widths and the frequency of the up and down sweeps.

■ How to Produce Interrupted Motion

Width: Relative to the last counter-cut added, the next counter-cut should be wider or narrower by 1½″ or more. The more contrast in counter-cut widths, the more interrupted the motion—like the outline of a city or a rocky ledge (Figure 10-9A).

Motion: You may go up or down at will with each counter-cut; there is no minimum number of counter-cuts in one direction. The shorter the sequence, the more jarring the motion.

NOTE: The last counter-cut of each sweep is also counted as the first counter-cut in the next sweep.

Figure 10-9B Interrupted Motion
Irregular thin and wide counter cuts

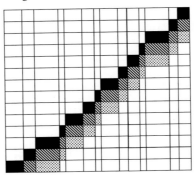

NOTE: You can combime both types of motion, progressive and interrupted, in the same Bargello quilt.

FULL, PARTIAL AND EXTENDED DROPS

As you create Bargello movement by adding counter-cuts, each counter-cut can move up or down by a full drop, or a partial drop. You can combine full and partial drops in one quilt.

In a *full drop* the next counter-cut is moved up or down a full strip height, so the seam junctions of all strata strips match at their corners (Figure 10-10). **All counter-cuts are opened on a seam.**

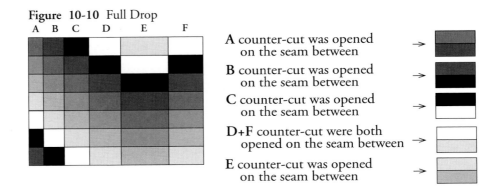

Figure 10-10 Full Drop

A counter-cut was opened on the seam between →

B counter-cut was opened on the seam between →

C counter-cut was opened on the seam between →

D+F counter-cut were both opened on the seam between →

E counter-cut was opened on the seam between →

In a *partial drop* the next counter-cut is moved up or down less than a full unit width, so the fabrics overlap slightly and the seam junctions don't intersect (Figure 10-11). Partial drops are useful if your strata has (sloppy) irregular seams, as you won't have to fuss trying to match seams. Partial drops are also useful for beginners who don't want to match seams. Every other counter-cut will be opened *on* a seam; the alternate counter-cuts will be opened by cutting a fabric piece in half .

NOTE: *Full drops* are the most dramatic and quickest type of drop. *Partial drops* soften and flatten the movement almost like finger painting over the edges. Look through the quilts for examples of each.

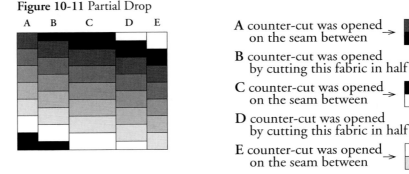

Figure 10-11 Partial Drop

A counter-cut was opened on the seam between →

B counter-cut was opened by cutting this fabric in half →

C counter-cut was opened on the seam between →

D counter-cut was opened by cutting this fabric in half →

E counter-cut was opened on the seam between →

CONSECUTIVE PATTERN VS VERTICAL INTERRUPTIONS

The Bargello pattern is *consecutive* if all the counter-cuts are sewn together after designing the Bargello (Figure 10-12).

Figure 10-12 Consecutive Pattern

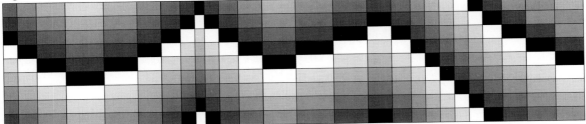

Vertical interruptions are fabric strips placed between the counter-cuts before they are sewn together (Figure 10-13A or B).

Vertical interruptions have tremendous design potential. After the counter-cuts are arranged in the Bargello design, vertical interruptions may be incorporated into the design *in the following ways:*

a) the strips of fabric may be sewn between every counter-cut, or

b) the locations of the interruptions may selectively chosen.

c) the same fabric may be used for all the interruptions, or

d) a variety of fabrics may be used.

e) light strips, called Icicles (Figure 10-13A)

f) dark strips, called Jail Bars (Figure 10-13B)

g) the interruptions may be a consistent width, or

h) many different widths.

i) the strips may also be pleated *or* 3-dimensional:

    1) for each interruption, a single fabric may be folded (Figure 10-14) or

    2) dual fabrics may be sewn together and folded on the seam to create different effects per side of the pleat (Figure 10-15).

Figure 10-13A Vertical Interuptions: Icicles

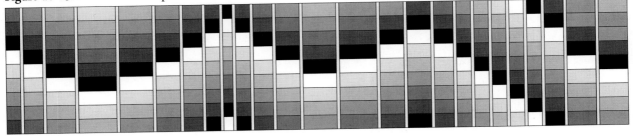

Figure 10-13B Vertical Interuptions: Jail Bars

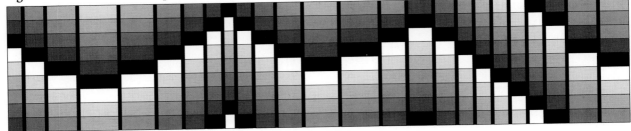

NOTE: **It is important to realize that whatever width of the vertical interruption strip you choose to insert, the width of the Bargello design increases by that same amount, less ½″ for seam allowances.** For example, if you add a 1″ strip between two counter-cuts you are adding ½″ to the finished width of the Bargello pattern. You must take these measurements into account as you plan the horizontal dimensions of your quilt.

One 45″ strata unit which is vertically interrupted between every counter cut usually maintains a 45″ wide size when it's sewn together and finished.

Vertical interruptions eliminate the need to match seams at the seam junctions. Because of this, they are a good way to work with irregular strata. They are also very powerful and dramatic. *I call dark interruptions jail bars or window bars, and light ones icicles.* A series of shaded values or dual fabric pleats will add extra drama and dimension to the vertical interruptions.

■ THREE-DIMENSIONAL PLEATS: VERTICAL INTERRUPTIONS

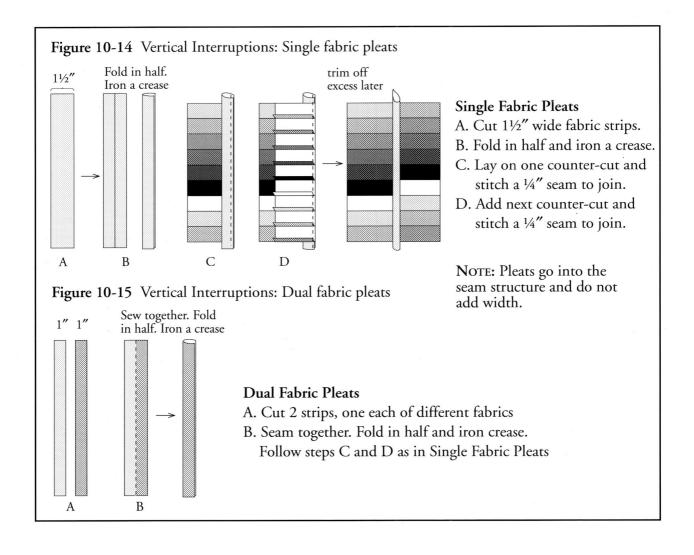

Figure 10-14 Vertical Interruptions: Single fabric pleats

1½″   Fold in half. Iron a crease   trim off excess later

A   B   C   D

Single Fabric Pleats

A. Cut 1½″ wide fabric strips.

B. Fold in half and iron a crease.

C. Lay on one counter-cut and stitch a ¼″ seam to join.

D. Add next counter-cut and stitch a ¼″ seam to join.

NOTE: Pleats go into the seam structure and do not add width.

Figure 10-15 Vertical Interruptions: Dual fabric pleats

1″ 1″   Sew together. Fold in half. Iron a crease

A   B

Dual Fabric Pleats

A. Cut 2 strips, one each of different fabrics

B. Seam together. Fold in half and iron crease.
   Follow steps C and D as in Single Fabric Pleats

■ Three-Dimensional Pleats: Arranging the Pleats

When stitching the borders or binding to a Bargello design with 3-dimensional pleats, it is necessary to take the top edge of the pleats and drag them all to the left or right (Figure 10-16). The bottom edge also needs to be dragged flat to the left or right. All of the pleats on one edge should go in the same direction.

The top and bottom can go in the same direction or they can go in opposite directions causing a natural twist midway in the 3-dimensional pleat (Figure 10-17). It is not necessary to tack the pleat.

Usually however, vertical 3-dimensional pleats must be tacked into position where you want to expose the Bargello fabrics (Figure 10-18). If the height of the Bargello design is over 20″, it is possible to get 2 tacks per pleat to create a double flow (Figure 10-19).

After the quilt top is sewn together and the batting, backing and quilting have been completed, fold and tack the pleats into their desired pattern. Use straight pins to try out several different flowing designs.

Figure 10-16

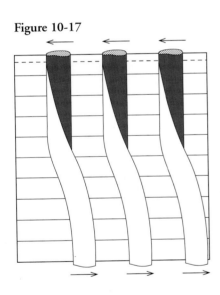

Figure 10-17

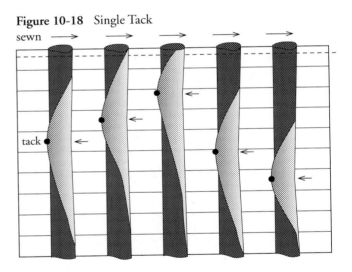

Figure 10-18 Single Tack

Figure 10-19 Double Tack

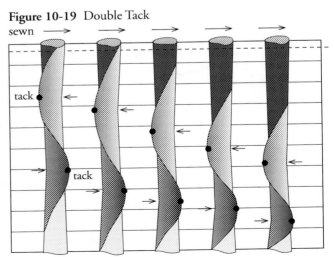

UNITS OF BARGELLO MOVEMENT

Figure 11-1A

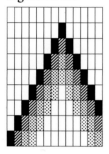

Figure 11-1B

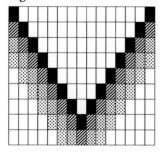

Figure 11-2

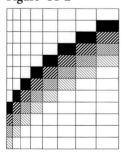

Figure 11-3

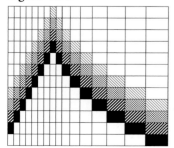

This chapter includes illustrated instructions on how to achieve different Bargello design effects. Study the photographs of the quilts in this book for examples of how these effects have been combined. Almost all Bargello quilts combine several elements, contrasting soft billowy mountains and S-curves with thin, piercing areas. The possibilities are infinite and the contrasts are exciting!

All of these use *design units* and are not created by one counter-cut alone. Use:

1) **a repetition of similar counter-cuts,** maintaining a counter-cut width for four or more counter-cuts. Any width can be repeated. For example, thin piercing areas use numerous counter-cuts that are thin. Together they create high, thin and piercing movement. Turned upside down the effect they have is deep, low and piercing. Again, these come from counter-cuts that are extremely thin and numerous, used side by side for 8 or more counter-cuts (Figure 11-1A & B).

2) **a gradation of increasing or decreasing counter-cut widths** For example, you can create a gradation by 1/2″ increments going from a 2½″ to a 2″ to a 1½″ to a 1″ to a 3/4″ (Figure 11-2), or

3) **use both repetition and stair-stepping** For example, enter a high peak or a deep piercing area with 8 of your thinnest cuts and then as you pull out of that, pull out differently than you entered it. If you created up motion with 1/2″ gradations, move in the opposite direction with 1″ gradations so that the sweep into the piercing area and the sweep out of it are not the same (Figure 11-3).

SWEEPS AND TRILLS

■ Sweeps

A sweep is any unit of motion between a high and low place (Figures 11-4A & 11-4B). Long sweeps or short sweeps are possible; effective Bargello quilts have three or more different-length sweeps, all working together (Figure 11-4C).

Figure 11-4A　　**Figure 11-4B**

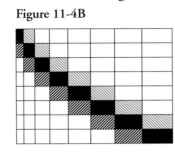

Figure 11-4C　Seven Sweeps

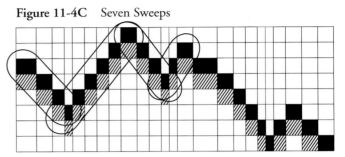

Figure 11-5　Trill added to a Sweep

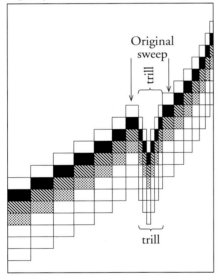

Original sweep

trill

trill

If you plan a long sweep into or out of a piercing thinness, it's pleasing to accent it by adding a little *trill*, a small interruption to a sweep. For instance, within a long sweep of counter-cuts, add two small sweeps of three or four counter-cuts in the opposite direction and then three to four more to catch back up with the original sweep for a total of six to seven thin counter-cuts (Figure 11-5).

■ S-Curves

An "S curve" is a very powerful element. It can be "thin–wide–thin" or "wide–thin–wide." Thin to thin will start with very thin cuts and have gradual increments toward an extremely wide cut, 2½ times the original strata strip width and graduating back downward to a thin cut (Figure 11-6). In other words, thin–wide–thin all in one downward or upward motion sweep.

The same thing is true if the wide cut is the beginning and a thin area is gradually reached, then gradually increased to another wide area, becoming a wide–thin–wide inverted S curve (Fig. 11-7). S-curves usually involve 9 to 23 counter-cuts to be dramatic and effective. An S- curve usually involves an odd number of counter-cuts hitting the thinnest or widest at its center.

NOTE: It is not essential for an S curve to be symmetrical, you can enter into the S motion with ¼″ gradations and you

Figure 11-6　S-Curve

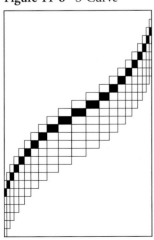

Figure 11-7　S-Curve

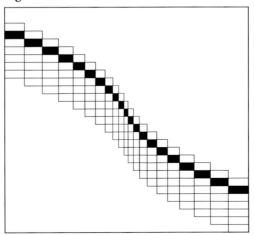

can pull out of it with ½" to 1" gradations. It is not essential that it is symmetrical, it's only essential that it starts and ends with similar widths, travels through a high contrast width, and all of the motion flows in one downward or upward sweep (i.e., one sweep).

■ Mountains and Meadows

Mountains and meadows are smooth, calm, billowy elements. Mountains go up (Figure 11-8A), and meadows go down (Figure 11-8B). The simplest mountain is a series of counter-cuts that are identical or get gradually wider for 5 to 7 (or more) counter-cuts as they go up, then downward for at least 5 to 7 (or more) counter-cuts. For a meadow, the counter-cuts first move downward, then upward. Mountains and meadows are both created by combining two sweeps. If the two sweeps

Figure 11-8A

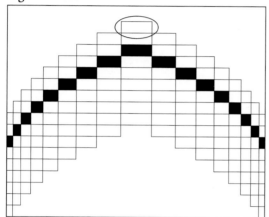

Figure 11-8B

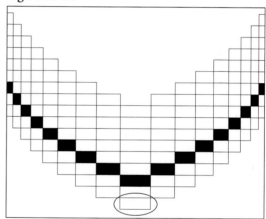

are the same, the effect is symmetrical (Figure 11-8A & B). If the sweeps are different, the effect is asymmetrical (Figure 11-9A & B).

Figure 11-9A

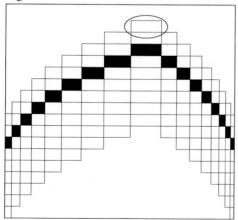

Figure 11-9B

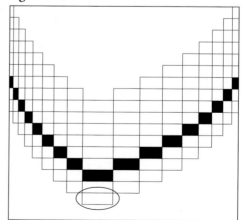

The number of counter-cuts and the rate at which the counter-cuts change in width affect the appearance of the design element. Graceful mountains are made by gradually changing to wider counter-cut widths. As you approach the top of the mountain make the counter-cuts

Figure 11-10

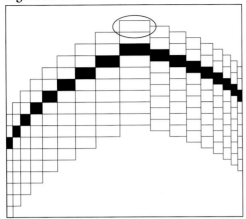

successively wider, with the widest counter-cut at the highest point. As you move down, make the counter-cuts successively narrower. Start downward and then go up to make a meadow.

a) The top of the mountain is the counter-cut "most high" in the motion sequence (see circled areas, Figures 11-8A & 11-9A). The movement can also be changed by half-staggers as you leave the top of the hill; this will slow the motion and make that area even softer and more billowy. (Figure 11-10, to the right of center, is slubbed.)

b) The bottom of the valley is the counter-cut "most low" in the motion sequence (Figures 11-8B & 11-9B).

NOTE: The top or bottom are not necessarily in the middle of the mountain or meadow.

On the other hand, if the counter-cuts are identical on both sides of the top of a mountain or the bottom of a meadow, the motion sequence is symmetrical even though the whole quilt may be asymmetrical (Figure 11-11).

To add interest and create an asymmetrical effect alter either a) the number of counter-cuts on one side, or b) the rate at which the counter-cut widths change, or c) both. For example, you could go up a hill with counter-cuts that increase ½″ increments, and go down the hill with counter-cuts that decrease in ¼″ increments, or even 1″ increments.

Figure 11-11

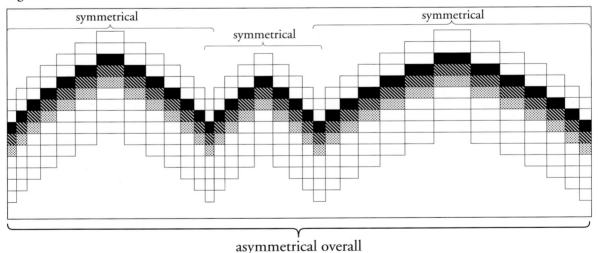

asymmetrical overall

■ Peaks and Spikes

A peak is created just like a mountain with one difference: instead of increasing in width, the counter-cuts decrease in width as the height of the peak is approached. On the other side of the peak the direction of the motion sweep is reversed and the counter-cuts gradually increase in width (Figure 11-12A). If a peak is pointing down, it is called a spike (Figure 11-12B).

Figure 11-12A Peak

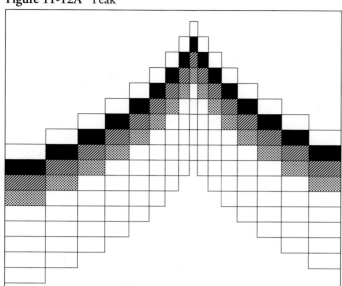

Figure 11-12B Spike

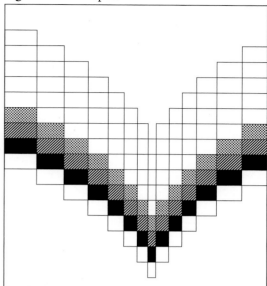

A spike is a very sharp, piercing element. The narrower the counter-cuts, the more piercing and dramatic the spike will appear.

If the counter-cuts are identical in size and number on both sides of the peaks and spikes, the effect will by symmetrical. To add interest and create asymmetry, you may alter either: a) the number of counter-cuts, or b) the rate at which the counter-cut widths change, or c) both.

■ S-curves

S-curves differ from mountains and meadows, and peaks and spikes in that the direction of the motion is either all upward or all downward; an S-curve is one sweep. There are two dramatic ways to make an S-curve — thin to wide to thin (Figure 11-13A), or the opposite, wide to thin to wide (Figure 11-13B)—all moving in one direction (all up or all down). The "drama" of an S-curve is produced by contrast in widths, it is the area at which the thinnest or widest contrast appears.

Figure 11-13A S-Curve

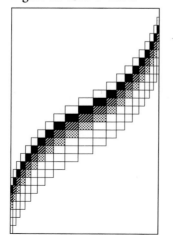

Figure 11-13B S-Curve

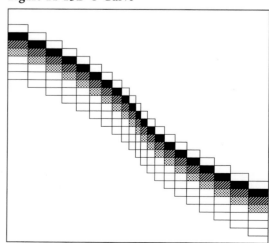

The number of counter-cuts used and the rate at which the counter-cuts increase and then decrease in width all affect the appearance of an S-curve.

If the counter-cuts are identical on both sides of the "drama" of an S-curve, it is symmetrical. You may wish to alter either of the number of counter-cuts on one side or the rate at which the counter-cut widths change or both to create an asymmetrical S-curve (Figure 11-14).

Figure 11-14

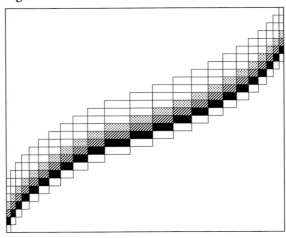

Figure 11-15

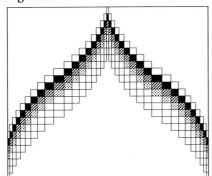

■ Wishbones

A wishbone is a peak formed by putting two S-curves together. An upward-pointing wishbone looks like the Taj Mahal (Figure 11-15). Wishbones are very graceful and are often used in symmetrical designs. They can be found in symmetrical or asymmetrical quilts (Figure 11-16).

Figure 11-16

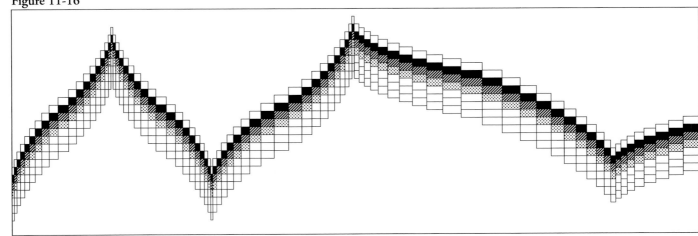

■ Trills

You may want to add a little interest to a long gentle sweep by adding a few thin counter-cuts. I call this interruption a trill. For example, a trill could be composed of three thin counter-cuts up and four thin counter-cuts back down in otherwise monotonous sweep. *Trills are usually added to dramatize uninteresting areas that have developed during the design process* (Figure 11-17).

Figure 11-17

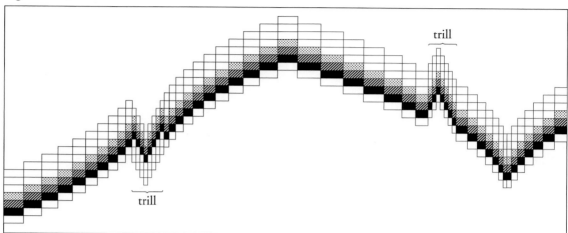

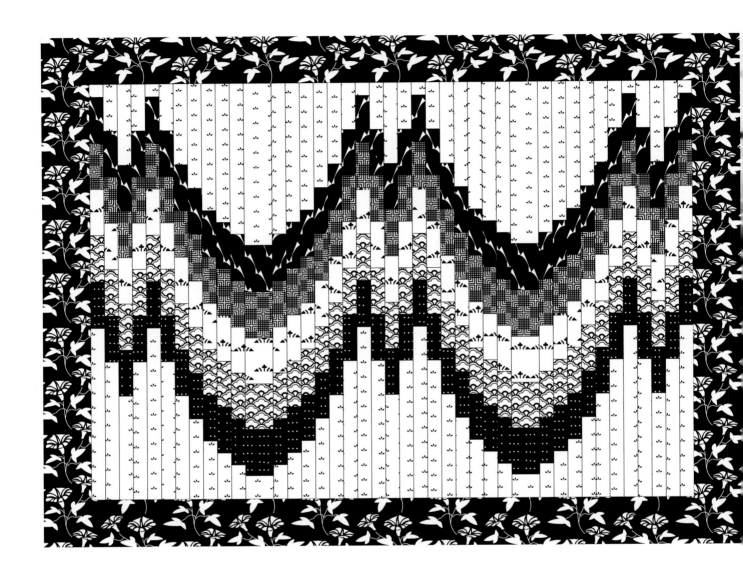

Reverse-repeat with Background Spacer
Symmetrical with partial drops or half staggers,
note the variety of half staggers used. They are
not consistent amounts.

CHAPTER 12

STRATA MATH
DESIGNING THE QUILT SIZE

If this chapter makes you nervous, try to relax and feel at ease. First, every quilt photographed has all of its yardage planned for you in Appendix B. Over 60 quilts can be made before any yardage calculations are required! Secondly, this chapter frees you of doing any calculations—the work has already been done for you. All you need to do is select the correct chart. Each chart presents a different type of information and all of the charts work together. The charts cover how tall your strata becomes, what size strip to use, the type of strata to choose, and how many strata to create. And remember, you can always make a quilt and then measure it to know the "real" size! As long as you don't need a specific size to fit a specific need, this is an excellent approach.

Very few quilters are excited about the math involved in planning a quilt, but every quilt requires some mathematical considerations, just because it has height and width. For some reason, when numbers and calculations are involved we feel that we are responsible for more than creating a beautiful quilt and become very intimidated. This anxiety is understandable; cloth is expensive and beautiful — we all want to use it well. The responsibility of being precise about calculations can separate us from our real passion: the beautiful effects of colors, values, and textures.

■ There are two different ways to use this chapter.

1. *Don't use the information at all.* Simply view the photographs and illustrations for inspiration and confidence, select fabrics, and then go directly to cutting and sewing strips. Make a tube, then make counter-cuts in a variety of widths, open the tubes to create up and down movement, and voilà . . . a Bargello Tapestry quilt. When you select this approach, you learn the size of your quilt and the look of your efforts after the fact! In this method, the knowledge happens after making the different choices.

This is a wonderful, carefree approach. It is the approach I used to create my first four Bargello Tapestry quilts. It is the best way to gain an initial understanding of the mathematical relationships between the height and width of the Bargello with regard to the strata used. This is the intuitive, flexible and spontaneous person's "get your feet wet quickly" approach. Read through these first two pages nevertheless—important details for everyone are discussed.

2. *Investigate all of the visual choices for strata styles, mathematical sizes and pattern flow before you cut your strips.* Read through every chapter, plan the strata style you prefer and your quilt size; then determine the yardage requirements for each fabric. The charts do all the work for you—all you need to do is select the correct chart for each consideration; number of fabrics, size of strips, and height and width of finished quilt. Calm, confident, "known" choices are possible with this approach.

THE MATH IN A NUTSHELL—FOR EVERYONE!

Figure 12-1

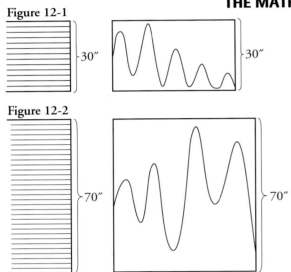

Figure 12-2

It is essential to have a basic understanding of Bargello motion and how it relates to the size of the strata unit. The height and width of a Bargello Tapestry quilt are determined by two things: the *height* of the strata unit and the *total number* of strata units used.

The height of the strata unit establishes the height of the Bargello quilt—and thus the height of the Bargello motion within the quilt. For example, if you want your Bargello Tapestry quilt to be 30″ tall, you must create a 30″ tall strata unit (Figure 12-1); for a 70″ tall quilt, you must create a 70″ tall strata unit (Figure 12-2).

The number of strata units establishes the possible width of the Bargello quilt—or how much Bargello pattern can be created to the left and right.

One strata produces 22″–28″ (average 25″) of sewn Bargello pattern (Figure 12-3A & 12-3B).

Two strata would average 50″ of sewn Bargello pattern (Figure 12-4A & 12-4B). Three strata would average 75″, four strata would average 100″, and so on.

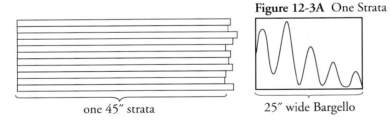

one 45″ strata

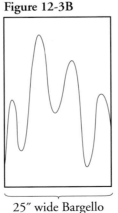

Figure 12-3A One Strata

25″ wide Bargello

Figure 12-3B

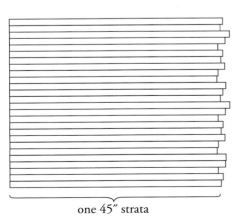

one 45″ strata

25″ wide Bargello

Figure 12-4A
This 50″ wide Bargello used two Strata

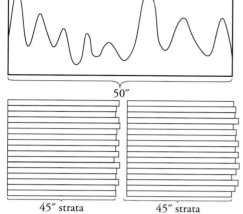

50″

45″ strata   45″ strata

Figure 12-4B

50″

45″ strata   45″ strata

NOTE: **The exception to this is a vertically interrupted quilt. A Bargello with vertical interruptions between every counter-cut keeps the 45" width per strata used.** With full vertical interruptions:
1 strata = 45" of sewn Bargello design,
2 strata = 90" of sewn Bargello design, and
3 strata = 135" of sewn Bargello design.

■ **Special Request**
Please take the Basic Quiz which follows, regardless of how much additional math information you plan to read. Understanding how the strata height determines the high and low motion of the Bargello movement is essential. Study the simple diagrams and then take the Basic Quiz to test yourself.

   The strata height determines the high and low movement of the Bargello pattern (Figure 12-5A&B). Even if the Bargello quilt is "sitting upright" the high and low motion can be detected. In Figure 12-5C it appears as side to side motion. This distinction is essential to planning your strata in order to achieve the desired results of Bargello motion over the surface of the quilt.

Figure 12-5C
strata height

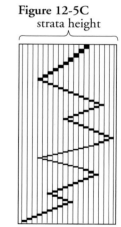

Figure 12-5A

strata height

Strata height=high and low motion

Figure 12-5B

rotates to:

■ **Basic Quiz**   *(Answers on page 121)*
Given Bargello designs 1 through 4 below, which edge of each design represents the strata height?

1. x or y
y

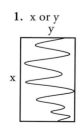

x

2. x or y
y

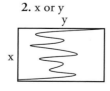

x

3. x or y
y

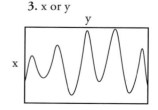

x

4. x or y
y

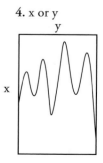

x

USING THE BARGELLO TABLES

HEIGHT

TABLE A (pages 76-77) shows the relationship between individual strip widths in a strata plan and the number of fabrics (positions) necessary to create the desired Bargello height of your quilt.

WIDTH

TABLE B (page 79) shows how many strata units you must make to create the Bargello width you desire.

NUMBER OF FABRICS

TABLE C (page 81) shows the number of strips to cut per fabric to make the necessary strata units, using the fabric arrangement you have already determined.

YARDAGE

TABLE D (pages 82-83) shows the actual yardage required of each fabric. (Spacers are not included.)

TABLE A – BARGELLO HEIGHT

Use Table A (pages 82-83) to plan your strata composition. Table A shows the relationship between the height of your quilt (shaded area), the number of fabric strips in the strata unit (along the top edge), and the cut or finished width of the individual strips (along the left edge). Of these three factors, you must decide two and then use the table to determine the third.

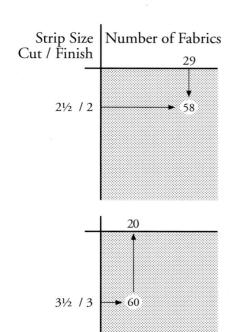

Example 1:
You like the look of a 2½″ cut strip (2″ finished) and want to use 29 fabric positions. Find 2½″ (2″) along the left edge and 29 along the top edge. The quilt height where these two lines intersect is 58″.

If 58″ is too tall or not tall enough, then make a change in either: a) the width of the strips, or b) the number of strips used.

Example 2:
You want your quilt to be 60″ tall and choose strips that are cut 3½″ wide (3″ finished). Find 3½″ (3″) along the left edge and 60″ in the shaded area. Your strata unit will require 20 fabric positions. (This could be 10 different fabrics repeated or reverse-repeated 2 times for a total of 20 positions or 20 different fabrics.)

If you want to use fewer or more fabric strips, then make a change to either: a) the quilt height, or b) the strip width used.

■ Quiz — Table A (Answers on page 121)

Two of the aspects are given. Determine the third using Table A.

1. Using a 3″ cut strip (2½″ finished) and 26 fabric positions, how tall is your Bargello quilt?

2. Using a 96″ Bargello height and 4½″ cut strips (4″ finished), how many fabric positions does the strata unit require?

3. Using a 90″ Bargello height and 18 fabric positions, how wide are the individual strips cut?

TABLE A

Number of Fabric Positions in the Strata Plan

INDIVIDUAL STRIP SIZE (in inches) Cut	Finish	6	7	8	9	10	11	12	13	14	15	16	17	18
1½	1	6	7	8	9	10	11	12	13	14	15	16	17	18
1¾	1¼	7½	8¾	10	11¼	12½	13¾	15	16¼	17½	18¾	20	21¼	22½
2	1½	9	10½	12	13½	15	16½	18	19½	21	22½	24	25½	27
2¼	1¾	10½	12¼	14	15¾	17½	19¼	21	22¾	24½	26¼	28	29¾	31½
2½	2	12	14	16	18	20	22	24	26	28	30	32	34	36
2¾	2¼	13½	15¾	18	20¼	22½	24¾	27	29¼	31½	33¾	36	38¼	40½
3	2½	15	17½	20	22½	25	27½	30	32½	35	37½	40	42½	45
3¼	2¾	16½	19¼	22	24¾	27½	30¼	33	35¾	38½	41¼	44	46¾	49½
3½	3	18	21	24	27	30	33	36	39	42	45	48	51	54
3¾	3¼	19½	22¾	26	29¼	32½	35¾	39	42¼	45½	48¾	52	55¼	58½
4	3½	21	24½	28	31½	35	38½	42	45½	49	52½	56	59½	63
4¼	3¾	22½	26¼	30	33¾	37½	41¼	45	48¾	52½	56¼	60	63¾	67½
4½	4	24	28	32	36	40	44	48	52	56	60	64	68	72
4¾	4¼	25½	29¾	34	38¼	42½	46¾	51	55¼	59½	63¾	68	72¼	76½
5	4½	27	31½	36	40½	45	49½	54	58½	63	67½	72	76½	81
5¼	4¾	28½	33¼	38	42¾	47½	52¼	57	61¾	66½	71¼	76	80¾	85½
5½	5	30	35	40	45	50	55	60	65	70	75	80	85	90
5¾	5¼	31½	36¾	42	47¼	52½	57¾	63	68¼	73½	78¾	84	89¼	94½
6	5½	33	38½	44	49½	55	60½	66	71½	77	82½	88	93½	99

All numbers in the shaded area are given in inches.

TABLE A

Number of Fabric Positions in the Strata Plan

INDIVIDUAL STRIP SIZE (in inches) Cut	Finish	19	20	21	22	23	24	25	26	27	28	29	30
1½	1	19	20	21	22	23	24	25	26	27	28	29	30
1¾	1¼	23¾	25	26¼	27½	28¾	30	31¼	32½	33¾	35	36¼	37½
2	1½	28½	30	31½	33	34½	36	37½	39	40½	42	43½	45
2¼	1¾	33¼	35	36¾	38½	40¼	42	43¾	45½	47¼	49	50¾	52½
2½	2	38	40	42	44	46	48	50	52	54	56	58	60
2¾	2¼	42¾	45	47¼	49½	51¾	54	56¼	58½	60¾	63	65¼	67½
3	2½	47½	50	52½	55	57½	60	62½	65	67½	70	72½	75
3¼	2¾	52¼	55	57¾	60½	63¼	66	68¾	71½	74¼	77	79¾	82½
3½	3	57	60	63	66	69	72	75	78	81	84	87	90
3¾	3¼	61¾	65	68¼	71½	74¾	78	81¼	84½	87¾	91	94¼	97½
4	3½	66½	70	73½	77	80½	84	87½	91	94½	98	101½	105
4¼	3¾	71¼	75	78¾	82½	86¼	90	93¾	97½	101¼	105	108¾	112½
4½	4	76	80	84	88	92	96	100	104	108	112	116	120
4¾	4¼	80¾	85	89¼	93½	97¾	102	106¼	110½	114¾	119	—	—
5	4½	85½	90	94½	99	103½	108	112½	117	—	—		
5¼	4¾	90¼	95	99¾	104½	109¼	114	118¾	—	—			
5½	5	95	100	102	110	115	120	—	—				
5¾	5¼	99¾	105	110¼	115½	—	—						
6	5½	104½	110	115½	—								

All numbers in the shaded area are given in inches.

TABLE A – Adjustments

Adjustments for Strata with a Spacer

If you plan to incorporate a spacer section in your Bargello design, it must be accounted for in the total strata height and calculations. This can be accomplished in either of two ways:

1. Use Table A to determine the quilt height without the spacer area, i.e. the number of fabric positions, and the width of the fabric strips. Then increase the quilt height by the width of the desired spacer strip; River, Island, or Background.

   Example: using a 3″ cut width (2½″ finished), with 26 fabric positions, and 65″ quilt height —

   Adding a 12″ river spacer would increase the quilt height to 77″. Adding a 30″ island spacer would increase the quilt height to 95″. Adding a 65″ background spacer would increase the quilt height to 130″.

2. Determine the final desired height of the quilt *including* the spacer, then use Table A.

   Example: using a 3″ cut width (2½″ finished), with 26 fabric positions including a 12″ spacer = 65″ quilt height —

   To adjust for a 12″ river spacer (less than half-strata height), subtract 12″ from 65″, which gives 53″. Use 53″ for the quilt height in Table A, and a 3″ cut width, 2½″ finished. The new number of fabric positions is 21.

   To adjust for an island spacer (half- to whole-strata in height), subtract 20″ from 65″, which gives 45″. With 3″ cut width, 2½″ finished, this would be 18 fabrics.

   To adjust for a background spacer (whole-strata height or greater), subtract 40″ from 65″ to yield 25″. With 3″ cut width, 2½″ finished, this will be 9 fabrics.

TABLE B

Use Table B to determine how many strata units are necessary to create a Bargello quilt of the width you desire.

TABLE B	
Horizontal Bargello Quilt Size (inches)	Number of Complete Strata Units Needed
22-28	1
29-56	2
57-84	3
85-112	4
113-140	5

Two of the quilts illustrated here, R and S, have similar dimensions but have different strata requirements.

Quilt R is 60″ tall and 45″ wide. It requires a strata unit 60″ tall. Using Table B, you can determine that two strata units would be required to create the 45″ in width.

Quilt S is 45″ tall and 60″ wide. It requires a strata unit 45″ tall. Using Table B, you can determine that three strata units would be required to create the 60" width.

Quilt T is of equal height and width.

Note: even if these quilts were turned such that (h) is at the top edge, (h) is still the strata height.

Quilt R

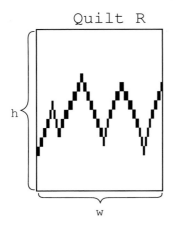

Quilt S

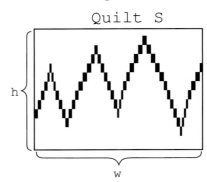

Quilt T

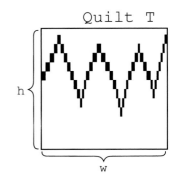

■ **Table B Quiz**   *(Answers on page 85)*

Use Table B and illustrations R, S, and T. For each quilt listed below:
  1) determine first whether it would look most like quilt R, S, or T above, then
  2) determine the strata height and
  3) the number of strata units required.

	Quilt dimensions	Quilt R, S or T?	strata height	# strata required
Quilt #1	50″ tall x 50″ wide	_____	_____	_____
Quilt #2	50″ tall x 72″ wide	_____	_____	_____
Quilt #3	72″ tall x 36″ wide	_____	_____	_____
Quilt #4	96″ tall x 96″ wide	_____	_____	_____
Quilt #5	60″ tall x 60″ wide	_____	_____	_____
Quilt #6	36″ tall x 24″ wide	_____	_____	_____
Quilt #7	24″ tall x 36″ wide	_____	_____	_____

TABLE C

Use Table C to determine how many strips to cut of each fabric.
   A. Select the type of strata sequence from the left edge of the chart.
   B. Then along the top of the chart, identify the number of strata units required (determined from Table B).
   C. Look in the shaded area for the number of strips required per fabric to create the total number of strata units needed.
      For actual yardage per fabric, use Table D (pages 82–83).

Table C

Type of Strata Sequence	Number of Strata Units Needed					
	1	2	3	4	5	6
Sequential	1	2	3	4	5	6
Double	2	4	6	8	10	12
Triple	3	6	9	12	15	18
Quadruple	4	8	12	16	20	24

Repeat or Reverse repeat

Sequential: each fabric is used only once in a strata unit
Double: the sequence of fabrics appears twice in the strata unit
Triple: the sequence of fabrics appears three times in the strata unit
Quadruple: the sequence of fabrics appears four times in the strata unit

NOTE: Double, triple, and quadruple strata may be repeat or reverse-repeat styles.
Example 1: If three strata units are needed and a sequential strata plan is used, then three strips of each fabric are required, i.e. one each per strata.

Example 2: If three strata units are needed and a triple strata plan is used, then nine strips of each fabric are required, i.e. three each per strata.

■ Quiz—Table C   *(Answers on page 121)*
1. You have a double repeat strata and need three strata units for the width, how many strips of each fabric are needed?

2. You have a sequential strata and need two strata units, how many strips of each fabric are needed?

3. You have a quadruple reverse-repeat and need two strata units, how many strips of each fabric are needed?

TABLE D

Number of Strips Required per Fabric

INDIVIDUAL STRIP SIZE (in inches) Cut Finish	1	2	3	4	5	6	7	8	9	10	11	12	13	14	15
1½ 1	1½	3	4½	6	7½	9	10½	12	13½	15	16½	18	19½	21	22½
1¾ 1¼	1¾	3½	5¼	7	8¾	10½	12¼	14	15¾	17½	19¼	21	22¾	24½	26¼
2 1½	2	4	6	8	10	12	14	16	18	20	22	24	26	28	30
2¼ 1¾	2¼	4½	6¾	9	11¼	13½	15¾	18	20¼	22½	24¾	27	29¼	31½	33¾
2½ 2	2½	5	7½	10	12½	15	17½	20	22½	25	27½	30	32½	35	37½
2¾ 2¼	2¾	5½	8¼	11	13¾	16½	19¼	22	24¾	27½	30¼	33	35¾	38½	41¼
3 2½	3	6	9	12	15	18	21	24	27	30	33	36	39	42	45
3¼ 2¾	3¼	6½	9¾	13	16¼	19½	22¾	26	29¼	32½	35¾	39	42¼	45½	48¾
3½ 3	3½	7	10½	14	17½	21	24½	28	31½	35	38½	42	45½	49	52½
3¾ 3¼	3¾	7½	11¼	15	18¾	22½	26¼	30	33¾	37½	41¼	45	48¾	52½	56¼
4 3½	4	8	12	16	20	24	28	32	36	40	44	48	52	56	60
4¼ 3¾	4¼	8½	12¾	17	21¼	25½	29¾	34	38¼	42½	46¾	51	55¼	59½	63¾
4½ 4	4½	9	13½	18	22½	27	31½	36	40½	45	49½	54	58½	63	67½
4¾ 4¼	4¾	9½	14¼	19	23¾	28½	33¼	38	42¾	47½	52¼	57	61¾	66½	71¼
5 4½	5	10	15	20	25	30	35	40	45	50	55	60	65	70	75
5¼ 4¾	5¼	10½	15¾	21	26¼	31½	36¾	42	47¼	52½	57¾	63	68¼	73½	78¾
5½ 5	5½	11	16½	22	27½	33	38½	44	49½	55	60½	66	71½	77	82½
5¾ 5¼	5¾	11½	17¼	23	28¾	34½	40¼	46	51¾	57½	63¼	69	74¾	80½	86¼
6 5½	6	12	18	24	30	36	42	48	54	60	66	72	78	84	90

The number in the shaded area is the exact quantity per fabric required and is given in inches.
Always add 4 - 9" extra when purchasing tollow for miscuts and shrinkage.

TABLE D

Number of Strips Required per Fabric

INDIVIDUAL STRIP SIZE (in inches) Cut Finish	16	17	18	19	20	21	22	23	24	25	26	27	28	29	30
1½ 1	24	25½	27	28½	30	31½	33	34½	36	37½	39	40½	42	43½	45
1¾ 1¼	28	29¾	31½	33¼	35	36¾	38½	40¼	42	43¾	45½	47¼	49	50¾	52½
2 1½	32	34	36	38	40	42	44	46	48	50	52	54	56	58	60
2¼ 1¾	36	38¼	40½	42¾	45	47¼	49½	51¾	54	56¼	58½	60¾	63	65¼	67½
2½ 2	40	42½	45	47½	50	52½	55	57½	60	62½	65	67½	70	72½	75
2¾ 2¼	44	46¾	49½	52¼	55	57¾	60½	63¼	66	68¾	71½	74¼	77	79¾	82½
3 2½	48	51	54	57	60	63	66	69	72	75	78	81	84	87	90
3¼ 2¾	52	55¼	58½	61¾	65	68¼	71½	74¾	78	81¼	84½	87¾	91	94¼	97½
3½ 3	56	59½	63	66½	70	73½	77	80½	84	87½	91	94½	98	101½	105
3¾ 3¼	60	63¾	67½	71¼	75	78¾	82½	86¼	90	93¾	97½	101¼	105	108¾	112½
4 3½	64	68	72	76	80	84	88	92	96	100	104	108	112	116	120
4¼ 3¾	68	72¼	76½	80¾	85	89¼	93½	97¾	102	106¼	110½	114¾	119	—	—
4½ 4	72	76½	81	85½	90	94½	99	103½	108	112½	117	—	—		
4¾ 4¼	76	80¾	85½	90¼	95	99¾	104½	109¼	114	118¾	—	—			
5 4½	80	85	90	95	100	105	110	115	120	—	—				
5¼ 4¾	84	89¼	94½	99¾	105	110¼	115½	—	—						
5½ 5	88	93½	99	104½	110	115½	—	—							

The number in the shaded area is the exact quantity per fabric required and is given in inches.
Always add 4 - 9" extra when purchasing tollow for miscuts and shrinkage.

TABLE D

After using Table C to determine the number of strips to cut for each fabric, use Table D to determine the yardage required per fabric. *Always add 4″-9″ extra to allow for shrinkage and miscuts.*

   A. Select the cut or finished width of the strips from the left edge of the chart.

   B. Locate the number of strips of each fabric required along the top of the chart.

   C. Then determine the exact number of inches of each fabric required from the shaded area. If the amount of fabric required doesn't appear in the chart, you will need less than ⅛ inch.

■ **Quiz—Table D**   *(Answers on page 85)*

Determine the yardage needed of each fabric.

1. The finished width of your strips is 2″, and you need 4 strips of each fabric.

2. The cut width of your strips is 4¾″, and you need 3 strips per fabric.

NOTE: **Be sure to multiply the spacer cloth amount by the number of strata units needed. There is no chart for spacer fabric requirements.**

ANSWERS

■ **Basic Quiz Answers:**

1. y = strata height   3. x = strata height
2. y = strata height   4. x = strata height

■ **Table A Quiz Answers**

1. 65″
2. 24 fabric positions
    if *sequential*—24 different fabrics
    if *repeated twice*—12 different fabrics
    if *reverse-repeated* two times—12 fabrics
    if repeated or reverse-repeated three times—
      8 different fabrics
3. 5½″ cut (5″ finished)

■ **Table B Quiz Answers**

1. T, 50″, 2 strata required
2. S, 50″, 3 strata required
3. R, 72″, 2 strata required
4. T, 96″, 4 strata required
5. T, 60″, 3 strata required
6. R, 36″, 1 strata required
7. S, 24″, 2 strata required

■ **Table C Quiz Answers**

1. 6 strips per fabric
2. 2 strips per fabric
3. 8 strips per fabric

■ **Table D Quiz Answers**

1. 10″ — purchase 1/3 yard of each fabric.
2. 14 ¼″—purchase 1/2 yard of each fabric.

A P P E N D I X   A

Glossary

Accordion pleating   Ironed creases that occur in the strata unit on the front side at the seams. Check the strata unit for pleats by gently pulling from top to bottom after ironing. Re-iron each strip to its full width if creases "pop open" near seam areas. See Chapter 7, **Strata Construction**.

Active fabrics   Fabrics that look busy because the print scale is large and/or there is high contrast (in color or value) between the design and the background.

Background spacer   A relatively wide strip of fabric added to the strata unit. When the Bargello design is constructed, the background spacer fabric appears both above and below the entire Bargello design. The design appears to float on the background spacer.

Clean-up cut   A cut which creates a 90° angle to cloth or quilt edges on strata units.

Cliff   An area of sharp contrast by value in the strata unit, where the light end of one run is connected to the dark end of another run.

Close-contrast   A method of fabric selection and arrangement in which there is little visual difference from one fabric to the next in a strata unit when viewed at a distance of 8 to 10 feet.

Double-voiced fabric   A fabric having two or more dominant colors or values, so that different 1″ areas of the fabric feature different colors and/or values.

Double-up   Two strips of the same fabric occurring side-by-side in the strata unit. Double-ups occur in prime reverse-repeat strata compositions.

Drop   The distance a counter-cut moves relative to the last counter-cut added to the design. A *full drop* is created when the next counter-cut is moved up or down the width of one fabric strip. A *partial drop* results when the next counter-cut is moved up or down less than one full strip height. A *slub* is when the next counter-cut moves up or down *more* than one fabric strip.

Flirting fabric A fabric with two distinct colors. It is found in one color area, not between two color areas. Thus the fabric flirts with the second color rather than "walking" between the two.

Full Drop A full drop is created when counter-cuts move up or down the width of one fabric strip.

Half Stagger Same as *partial drop*.

Hill A sequence of dark fabrics where the dark ends of two runs come together.

Interrupted motion The effect of breaking up the waves of the Bargello design by: 1) sharply increasing or decreasing the width of the next counter-cut, and/or 2) having relatively few counter-cuts within each up or down motion sweep, and/or 3) moving up or down more than a single seam drop from one counter-cut to the next. See Chapter 10, **Bargello Pattern Flow.**

Island spacer A strip of fabric wider than the others in the strata unit, visually cutting apart and yet surrounding and separating large areas of Bargello design.

Lacy An active visual effect created by the use of similarly colored fabrics which range from dark to light due to change in the density of print scale.

Lettuce leaves A distortion in the strata unit that makes the outside edges (strips) ripple slightly; usually involving first and last strips only. See also Roller Coaster edges.

Motion The apparent movement within the Bargello design created by the placement of each counter-cut, up or down relative to the last counter-cut.

Overlap A fabric flow that occurs whenever the seams in the counter-cuts are not matched corner to corner of themselves. All spacers (river, island, and background) overlap, as well as Bargello designs with partial drops from counter-cut to counter-cut.

Partial Drop   A partial drop is created when counter-cuts move up and down less than the width of one fabric strip.

Print scale   The relative size of the pattern printed on a fabric. In a large-scale print, a 2″ square area of the fabric may be very different from another 2″ area. In a medium-scale print, 1″ square areas will be different. In a small-scale print, 1/2″ square areas will be similar.

Progressive motion   Smooth Bargello motion that is created by (1) maintaining a gradual change in the width of the counter-cuts, and/or (2) having three or more counter-cuts in each up or down motion sweep.

Rainbow   Distortion of the strata unit which causes it to curve into a rainbow (arched) shape. See Chapter 7, **Strata Construction.**

Repeat   A sequence of fabric strips in the strata unit repeated in the same order, as in fabrics 1 through 8 followed by fabrics 1 through 8 again.

Reverse-repeat (contrived)   A reverse-repeat strata unit in which the first and last fabrics of a sequence of fabric strips are not repeated. An example of 8 fabrics reverse-repeated in a contrived fashion would be fabrics 1 through 8 followed by fabrics 7 through 2.

Reverse-repeat (prime)   A reverse-repeat strata unit in which a sequence of fabric strips are repeated in full in their reverse order, as in fabrics 1 through 8 followed by fabrics 8 through 1. Fabrics 1 and 8 create *double-ups.*

River spacer   A strip of fabric somewhat wider than the others in the strata unit. It will overlap itself in the Bargello pattern development and look like a river running through the Bargello design. It does not alter the design as much as a Background Spacer or an Island Spacer.

Roller Coaster Edges   A distortion in the strata unit that is like *lettuce leaves,* but more exaggerated. Ripples are at the edge of the strata strips and often involve several rows of strips at the top and bottom edges.

Run   A sequence of fabric strips in the strata unit, arranged in a light to dark gradation by any of the following: color, value, and/or print scale.

Scroll   The visual movement of each individual fabric in the Bargello design, as it disappears off the top or bottom edge and immediately reappears on the opposite edge. Movement of fabrics from the top or bottom edge to the opposite edge.

Slope   A distortion of the beginning end of a strata unit. The edge of the strata is not at a 90° angle to the internal seams of the strata.

Slub   The movement of a counter-cut when it drops more than one fabric width relative to the counter-cut next to it.

Spacer   A strip of fabric wider than the others in the strata unit. See River spacer, Background spacer, and Island spacer.

Stair step   To use the same counter-cut width for three or more counter-cuts placed side by side.

Strata unit   A fabric unit made by sewing two or more strips of fabric together along their long edges.

Sweep   A series of counter-cuts in which the Bargello design moves from a high point to a low point, or vice versa.

Talking fabric   A fabric with two or more "voices" i.e., two distinct colors or values. Same as *walking fabric* and *flirting fabric*.

Torque   A twist in a strata unit or Bargello Tapestry quilt caused by irregularity in sewing. To eliminate the torque, trim to a 90° angle using an internal seam. For strata, the accurate seam is a horizontal seam. For the Bargello quilt, the accurate seam is a vertical seam. See Chapter 7, **Strata Construction.**

Trill   Two sharp, small Bargello sweeps (3 to 4 counter-cuts per sweep), contained within a larger single sweep, forming a dramatic accent against the large sweep.

Tubed   A strata unit is tubed when the top and bottom strips are sewn together along their long edges. This is done before counter-cutting the strata and after the 90° angle is created. It cannot be done until *slope, rainbows,* and *lettuce leaves* are eliminated.

Valley   A sequence of light fabrics where the light ends of two runs meet.

Value   The visual impression of a fabric to be dark, medium or light. Value is relative; it is always determined by the contrast between two fabrics.

Walking fabric   A fabric that includes two or more colors or values, so that some areas are dominated by one aspect and other areas feature another aspect. Used as a bridge between two runs that feature different colors or different values. See also "lacy."

Worked upon itself   A Bargello Tapestry design without a spacer section.

A P P E N D I X   B

Yardage and Cutting Information for Quilts in Color Gallery

SEQUENTIAL

1
Southwest Canyon
(from Grand Canyon Series)
62" x 44"
by Louise Harris
sequential
asymmetrical w/ interrupted
motion
41 fabrics: 1/8 yd each
    cut 2 strips ea fabric: 2¼" x 45"
2 strata units

2
Lamé à la Bargello
28" x 48"
by Diane Becka
sequential
asymmetrical
24 fabrics: 1/8 yd each
    cut 2 strips ea fabric: 1½" x 45"
2 strata units

3
Magic Mountains
84" x 49"
by Louise Harris
sequential
asymmetrical
27 fabrics: 1/8 yd each
    cut 2 strips ea fabric: 1½" x 45"
2 strata units

4
Double Valance S Curve
26" x 56"
by Marilyn Doheny
sequential
asymmetrical
26 fabrics: 1/8 yd each
    cut 2 strips ea fabric: 1½" x 45"
2 strata units

4b.
Double Valance S Curve
Fabric Detail

5
Majesty
46" x 55"
by Donna Van Buren
sequential
asymmetrical
23 fabrics: 1/4 yd each
    cut 2 strips ea fabric: 2½" x 45"
2 strata units

6
Monet's Garden
36" x 56"
by Rhoda Lonergan
sequential
asymmetrical
19 fabrics: 1/4 yd each
    cut 2 strips ea fabric: 2" x 45"
2 strata units

7
Flower Garden
18" x 25"
by Alice Rudolph
sequential
asymmetrical
15 fabrics: 1/4 yd each
    cut 2 strips ea fabric: 2½" x 45"
2 strata units

8
Asphalt Jungle
60½" x 49"
by Vivian Larson
sequential
asymmetrical
20 fabrics: 1/4 yd each
    cut 2 strips ea fabric: 2¼" x 45"
2 strata units

SEQUENTIAL

9
Sparkling Water
21″ x 30″
by Sally Lindman
sequential
asymmetrical
14 fabrics: 1/4 yd each
   cut 1 strip ea fabric: 1½″ x 45″
1 strata unit

10
Garden Arches
20″ x 40″
by Marilyn Doheny
sequential
symmetrical
20 fabrics: 1/8 yd each
   cut 2 strips ea fabric: 1½″ x 45″
2 strata units

11
Fish Ladder
45″ x 60″
by Catherine Garvin
sequential
asymmetrical
20 fabrics: 1/4 yd each
   cut 2 strips ea fabric: 2″ x 45″
(some fabrics are used more
  than once)
2 strata units

12
First Ascent
38″ x 56″
by Robin Teal
sequential
asymmetrical
16 fabrics: 1/4 yd each
   cut 2 strips ea fabric: 2½″ x 45″
2 strata units

13
Yin Yang
25″ x 25″
by Diane Becka
sequential
asymmetrical
14 fabrics: 1/8 yd each
   cut 1 strip ea fabric: 2″ x 45″
1 strata unit

14
Anniversary Blessings
King size
by Robin Strobel
Fabric detail only
(whole quilt not shown)

REPEAT

15
Painted Desert
37″ x 65″
by Maribeth Donner
double repeat
asymmetrical
9 fabrics: 1/3 yd each
    cut 4 strips: 2″ x 45″
2 strata units

16
My Pink Garden
33″ x 26″
by Marilyn Doheny
double repeat
symmetrical
11 fabrics: 1/4 yd each
    cut 2 strips: 2″ x 45″
1 strata unit

17
Matilda's Music
80″ x 70″
by Joan Blair,
    owned by MaryAnn Schmidt
double repeat
asymmetrical
8 fabrics: 1 yd each
    cut 6 strips: 5½″ x 45″
3 strata units (1/2 stagger)

18
Cherry Pie
33″ x 35″
by Helen Wichern
double repeat
asymmetrical
9 fabrics: 1/4 yd each
    cut 2 strips: 2″ x 45″
1 strata unit

19
Candy Mountains
46″ x 30″
by Patsi Hanseth
double repeat
asymmetrical
10 fabrics: 1/4 yd each
    cut 2 strips: 2½″ x 45″
1 strata unit (1/2 stagger)

20.
Sweetness & Light
45″ x 55″
by Betty Ores
double repeat
symmetrical
13 fabrics: 1/3 yd each
    cut 4 strips: 2″ x 45″
2 strata units

21
Blue Mood
46″ x 56″
by Laurie Taylor
double repeat
asymmetrical
10 fabrics: 1/3 yd each
    cut 4 strips: 2½″ x 45″
2 strata units

22
Noël
30″ x 33″
by Marilyn Doheny
double repeat
asymmetrical
11 fabrics: 1/8 yd each
    cut 2 strips: 1½″ x 45″
1 strata unit

23
That Old Yin Yang
40″ x 45″
by Janet Kime
1 printed stripe fabric: 2 yds
tubed and shifted

REVERSE REPEAT

24
Madame Butterfly
44″ x 44″
by Marilyn Doheny
Prime Reverse repeat
asymmetrical
9 fabrics: 1/4 yd each
   cut 2 strips ea fabric: 2″ x 45″
1 strata unit

25
From Issaquah with Love
46″ x 40″
Artist unknown
Compromised Reverse repeat
asymmetrical with Island spacer
9 fabrics: 1/4 yd each
   cut 2 strips ea fabric: 2½″ x 45″
1 spacer cloth: 1/2 yd
   cut 1 strip: 10½″x 45″
1 strata unit

25b
From Issaquah with Love
Detail

26
My River In The Forest
45″ x 50″
by Marjorie Lorant
Compromised Reverse repeat
asymmetrical with Background
spacer   9 fabrics: 1/3 yd
each
   cut 4 strips ea fabric: 2½″ x 45″
1 spacer cloth: 1¼ yd
   cut 2 strips: 18½″x 45″
2 strata units

26b
My River In The Forest
Detail

RIVER SPACER

27
Desert Palisades
50″ x 70″ (front cover)
by Shelley Nelson
sequential with River spacer
asymmetrical
19 fabrics: 1/4 yd each
   cut 3 strips: 2″ x 45
1 spacer cloth: 2 yd
   cut 3 strip: 20½″ x 45″
3 strata units

28
Blue Arches
40″ x 55″
by Mary Beth Donner
repeated with River spacer
symmetrical
14 fabrics: 1/2 yd each
   cut 4 strips: 2½″ x 45″
1 spacer cloth: 1/2 yd
   cut 2 strips: 6½″ x 45″
2 strata units

29
Birds In Flight
35″ x 50″
by Susan Gordon
sequential with River spacer
(half staggers)
asymmetrical
12 fabrics: 1/4 yd each
   cut 2 strips: 2″ x 45″
1 spacer cloth: 1¼ yd
   cut 2 strips: 9½″ x 45″
2 strata units

30
Delicate Sensations
90″ x 70″
by Stephanie Newman
repeated with 2 River spacers
asymmetrical
18 fabrics: 1/2 yd each
   cut 4 strips: 2½″ x 45
1st spacer cloth: 1/3 yd
   cut 2 strips: 4½″ x 45″
2nd spacer cloth: 1/2 yd
   cut 2 strips: 6½″ x 45″
2 strata units

31
Misty Morning Memories of Monet
50″ x 59″
by Vivian Heiner
sequential with River spacer
asymmetrical
27 fabrics: 1/4 yd each
   cut 2 strips: 1½″ x 45″
1 spacer cloth: 1/2 yd
   cut 2 strips: 6½″ x 45″
2 strata units

32
Mountain Waterfall
90″ x 80″
by Leone Newman
sequential with River spacer
asymmetrical
19 fabrics: 1/2 yd each
   cut 3 strips: 4½″ x 45″
1 spacer cloth: 1¼″ yd
   cut 3 strips: 12½″ x 45″
3 strata units

RIVER SPACER (continued)

33
Red River Valley
15″ x 30″
by Marilyn Doheny
sequential with River spacer
asymmetrical
10 fabrics: 1/4 yd each
    cut 1 strip: 1½″ x 45″
1 spacer cloth: 1/4 yd
    cut 1 strip: 5½″ x 45″
1 strata unit

34 and Back Cover
Midnight at the Oasis
38″ x 38″
by Nell Moynihan
sequential with 2 River Spacers
asymmetrical
12 fabrics: 1/8 yd each
    cut 1 strip: 2½″ x 45″
1st spacer cloth: 1/2 yd
    cut 1 strip: 8½″ x 45″
2nd spacer cloth: 1/4 yd
    cut 1 strip: 3½″ x 45″
palm tree: 1/4 yd
1 strata unit

35
Contemporary Images
22″ x 52″
by Evie Newell
sequential with River spacer
asymmetrical
10 fabrics: 1/4 yd each
    cut 2 strips: 2″ x 45″
1 spacer cloth: 1/3 yd
    cut 2 strips: 5½″ x 45″
2 strata units

36
Presidential Suite
15″ x 30″
by Eloise Benedict
sequential with River spacer
asymmetrical
10 fabrics: 1/8 yd each
    cut 1 strip: 1½″ x 45
1 spacer cloth: 1/8 yd
    cut 1 strip: 5½″ x 45″
1 strata unit

37
Heat Wave
60″ x 55″
by Nancy Mahoney
sequential with 2 River spacers
asymmetrical
34 fabrics: 1/4 yd each
    cut 2 strips: 2″ x 45″
1st spacer cloth: 2/3 yd
    cut 2 strips: 10½″ x 45″
2nd spacer cloth: 1/3 yd
    cut 2 strips: 4½″ x 45″
2 strata units

38
Crazy Days of Summer or
Upstream Salmon
30″ x 36″
by Nell Clinton-Moynihan
sequential with River spacer
asymmetrical
12 fabrics:1/8 yd each
    cut 1 strip: 1½″ x 45
1 spacer cloth: 1/4 yd
    cut 1 strip: 6½″ x 45″
1 strata unit

BACKGROUND SPACER

39
Christmas Banner
50″ x 100″
by Marilyn Doheny and
   Sue Pilarski
sequential with Background spacer
asymmetrical
18 fabrics: 1/2 yd each
   cut 4 strips ea fabric: 2½″ x 45″
1 spacer cloth: 4 yd
   cut 4 strips: 30½″ x 45″
4 strata units

40
Untitled
50″ x 50″
by Janet Kime
asymmetrical with Background
spacer   1 stripe fabric:
(approx.) 1 yd
   cut 2 units (on fold): 22″ x 45″
1 spacer cloth: 1/4 yd
   cut 2 strips: 18½″ x 45″
2 strata units

41
Heart Monitor
55″ x 65″
by Mary E. Fox
Reverse repeat with Background
   spacer
asymmetrical
9 fabrics: 1/3 yd each
   cut 4 strips ea fabric: 2″ x 45″
1 spacer cloth: 1⅔ yd
   cut 2 strips: 26½″ x 45″
2 strata units

42
Reflections of Lahaina
38″ x 55″
by Diane Strand
sequential with Background spacer
asymmetrical
9 fabrics: 1/4 yd each
   cut 2 strips ea fabric: 2½″ x 45″
1 spacer cloth: 1¼ yd
   cut 2 strips: 18½″ x 45″
2 strata units

43
Larry's Dream
55″ x 75″
by Joel Patz
sequential with Background spacer
asymmetrical
17 fabrics: 1/4 yd each
   cut 2 strips ea fabric: 2½″ x 45″
1 spacer cloth: 2 yd
   cut 2 strips: 30½″ x 45″
2 strata units

44
My Purple Valances
27″ x 30″
by Marilyn Doheny
repeat with Background spacer
asymmetrical
8 fabrics: 1/3 yd each
   cut 4 strips ea fabric: 1½″ x 45″
1 spacer cloth: 1 yd
   cut 2 strips: 14½″ x 45″
2 strata units

45
Ooh La La
52″ x 64″
by Diane Becka
sequential with Background spacer
asymmetrical
13 fabrics: 1/4 yd each
   cut 2 strips ea fabric: 2½″ x 45″
1 spacer cloth: 2 yd
   cut 2 strips: 26½″ x 45″
2 strata units

ISLAND SPACER

46
Harbor Grays
44″ x 58″
by Vivian Heiner
sequential with Island spacer
16 fabrics: 1/4 yd each
   cut 2 strips: 2½″ x 45″
1 spacer fabric: 2/3 yd
   cut 2 strips: 9½″ x 45″
2 strata units

47
A River Runs Through It
38″ x 30″
by Sheila Hopkins
sequential with Island spacer
10 fabrics: 1/8 yd each
   cut 1 strip: 2½″ x 45″
1 spacer fabric: 1/2 yd
   cut 1 strip: 12½″ x 45″
1 strata unit

48
From Grand Forks, B.C.
66″ x 96″
by Emilie Belak
sequential with 2 spacers
19 fabrics: 1/4 yd each
   cut 3 strips: 2″ x 45″
1st (river) spacer fabric: 1/2 yd
   cut 2 strips: 6½″ x 45″
2nd (island) spacer fabric: 2/3 yd
   cut 2 strips: 10½″ x 45″
3 strata units

49
Spinning My Dreams
40″ x 60″
by Ola Booknight
sequential with Island spacer
12 fabrics: 1/4 yd each
   cut 2 strips: 2″ x 45″
1 spacer fabric: 1 yd
   cut 2 strips: 16½″ x 45″
2 strata units

50
Above The Fruited Plains
45″ x 55″
by Rhoda Lonergan
sequential with Island spacer
28 fabrics: 1/4 yd each
   cut 2 strips: 1½″ x 45″
1 spacer fabric: 2/3 yd
   cut 2 strips: 10½″ x 45″
2 strata units

51
Joan Loves Red
30″ x 45″
by Dawn Coons
sequential with Island spacer
12 fabrics: 1/4 yd each
   cut 2 strips: 2″ x 45″
1 spacer fabric: 2/3 yd
   cut 2 strips: 8½″ x 45″
2 strata units

52
May God Grant Prayers
72″ x 72″
by Lynn Boland
sequential with Island spacer
23 fabrics: 1/3 yd each
   cut 2 strips: 3″ x 45″
1 spacer fabric: 1 yd
   cut 2 strips: 15½″ x 45″
1 strata unit

53
Kabouki Island
48″ x 48″
by Marilyn Doheny
sequential with Island spacer
10 fabrics: 1/4 yd each
   cut 2 strips: 2″ x 45″
1 spacer fabric: 1/2 yd
   cut 1 strip: 12½″ x 45″
1 strata unit

54
My Floral Jungle
45″ x 30″
by Arlene Schekler
sequential with Island spacer
10 fabrics: 1/8 yd each
   cut 2 strips: 2″ x 45″
1 spacer fabric: 1/3 yd
   cut 1 strip: 8½″ x 45″
1 strata unit

VERTICAL INTERRUPTION

55
#1 Son
80″ x 70″
by Rhoda Lonergan
sequential with 1 River spacer
asymmetrical with
    Vertical interruptions
20 fabrics: 1/3 yd each
    cut 2 strips ea fabric: 3½″ x 45″
1st spacer: 1/2 yd
    cut 9½″ x 45″
black fabric for
    Vertical interruptions: 1/2 yd
1 strata unit

56
Graded Bars
51″ x 55″
by Diane Becka
sequential with Vertical interruptions
asymmetrical
34 fabrics: 1/8 yd each
    cut 2 strips ea fabric: 2″ x 45″
assorted fabrics for
    Vertical interruptions: 1/8 yd
each
1 strata unit

57
Fire & Ice On My Bed
120″ x 120″
by Maribeth Donner
sequential with Vertical interruptions
asymmetrical
56 fabrics: 1/4 yd each
    cut 2 strips ea fabric: 2½″ x 45″

black & red fabric for
    Vertical interruptions: 1/2 yd
each
2 strata units

58
Rory's Jungle Quilt
50″ x 76″
by Muriel Neale
sequential with Vertical interruptions
asymmetrical
13 fabrics: 1/3 yd each
    cut 2 strips ea fabric: 3½″ x 45″
assorted fabrics for
    Vertical interruptions: 1/8 yd
each
2 strata units

59
Jonathan L.S.
60″ x 66″
by Vivian Heiner
Reverse repeat with 2 River spacers
asymmetrical with Vertical
    interruptions
12 fabrics: 1/4 yd each
    cut 2 strips ea fabric: 2″ x 45″
1st spacer: 1/2 yd

cut 12″ x 45″
2nd spacer: 1/4 yd
    cut 5″ x 45″
assorted fabrics for
    Vertical interruptions: 1/8 yd
each
1 strata unit

60
Amazing Grace
25″ x 40″
by Vivian Heiner
sequential with 2 spacers and
    Vertical pleats
asymmetrical
10 fabrics: 1/4 yd each
    cut 2 strips ea fabric: 2″ x 45″
1st River spacer: 1/2 yd
    cut 4″ x 45″
2nd pop-corn spacer: 1/8 yd
    cut 1½″ x 45″
Medium pleat: 1/2 yd
    cut 13 strips: 1″ x 45″
Light to dark pleats: 1/8 yd ea
    cut 1 strip ea fabric: 1″ x 45″
2 strata units